A Technology Marketing Corporation Publication

Scriptwriting

For Effective Telemarketing

The Guide to Successful Business by Telephone

By Judy McKee ● Foreword by Nadji Tehrani

The Statement/Question Technique℠ is a registered servicemark of McKee Motivation Inc.

Cover design by Mary Beth D'Arcangelo

PRINTED IN THE UNITED STATES OF AMERICA

To order

Scriptwriting For Effective Telemarketing

call **800-243-6002** or **203-852-6800**

or fax **203-853-2845** or **203-838-4070**

Write to **Technology Marketing Corporation,
One Technology Plaza, Norwalk, CT 06854**

ISBN 0-936840-12-9

LIBRARY OF CONGRESS 93-61034

Published by
Technology Marketing Corporation
Also publisher of Telemarketing® magazine
One Technology Plaza, Norwalk, CT 06854 USA
203-852-6800 or **800-243-6002** Fax: **203-853-2845** or **203-838-4070**

INSPIRATION FOR WRITING THIS BOOK

As a telemarketing trainer and motivational speaker, my focus is on the human element of the telemarketing profession. My philosophy is: **the customer comes first**.

At the same time, the problems and feelings of the salesperson, telemarketer or customer service representative must be considered. The human factor is present on both sides of the telephone transaction, and the experience must be rewarding for each of the participants.

Many businesspeople who are contemplating or just beginning telemarketing are not satisfied with their initial results.

For most people, the major driving force is to increase sales and profits through effective performance of their telemarketing activities. They need advice on what to say and how to say it in a way that will make their business ventures more successful. They want help in writing their own effective scripts, or they want someone to write an effective script for them.

This book is written to assist anyone who makes or takes calls and is preparing to write telemarketing scripts. It will guide you to successful closure of telephone sales.

This book is a teaching instrument. The supervisors, managers and owners of businesses who do not know where to begin can start here. Others who have been successfully telemarketing for years may find a fresh approach that will lead to greater success and satisfaction in their interaction with prospects and customers.

The purpose of this book is not just "how to get the customer to buy." It encompasses the whole picture: how to get the customer to buy; how to maintain company and personal integrity; and how to keep CSRs and TSRs proud and satisfied with what they are doing.

It is my contention that the only effective scripts are those based on fairness, integrity, honesty, dignity, service and quality. The public is becoming more enlightened, causing business trends and personal values to shift from the glitter of the "personality ethic."

My scriptwriting technique is the result of having made thousands of telephone sales calls over the last 20 years or so. I have been using telemarketing, both inbound and outbound, as the prime method of promoting and sustaining my business.

As a telemarketing and training consultant, I have monitored innumerable calls and coached hundreds of TSRs and CSRs to assist them in achieving greater productivity and gaining self-assurance. Through trial and error, I have found what works and what doesn't work. You are welcome to take advantage of my experience and avoid making costly errors when preparing a script.

To fully understand my scriptwriting and training philosophy, I heartily recommend reading Stephen Covey's magnificent work entitled The 7 Habits of Highly Effective People, *a Fireside Book published by Simon and Schuster. This book is a revelation of ethics and their relationship to effectiveness.*

It is my intention that all who read this book will find the information, ideas, techniques and inspiration needed to become masterful scriptwriters for successful business by telephone. ☎

TABLE OF CONTENTS

Section   **Page**

FOREWORD   IX

INTRODUCTION   1
▶ TRADITIONAL SCRIPT/NEW AGE SCRIPT   5

Chapter I   THE TELEMARKETING INDUSTRY GROWS UP   7
             (But Not Without Pain)

Chapter II   PRE-SCRIPT PLANNING   11
             ▶ MENTAL PREPARATION   11
             ▶ DEFINITION OF PURPOSE   11
             ▶ DEFINING THE OBJECTIVES   12
                ☆ Primary Objectives   12
                ☆ Secondary Objectives   13
             ▶ QUALIFYING THE PROSPECT   13
             ▶ POTENTIAL OBSTACLES AND OBJECTIONS   16
             ▶ EXPECTED CHALLENGES   17
             ▶ COMPETITIVE ADVANTAGES AND BENEFITS   17
             ▶ DEFINE THE INITIAL OFFER   18
             ▶ DEFINE THE FALL-BACK OFFER   19
             ▶ CREATE A FORM   19
             ▶ SAMPLE PRE-SCRIPTWRITING PLANNING SHEET   21

Chapter III THE STATEMENT/QUESTION TECHNIQUE:
             NEVER MAKE THE CLIENT FEEL WRONG OR STUPID   23
             ▶ INITIATE A DIALOG   24
             ▶ CONTROL THE CALL, NOT THE PROSPECT
               OR CUSTOMER   25
             ▶ TSR CONFIDENCE BUILDER   25
             ▶ HOW IT WORKS   25

☆ *Sequence for Outbound Calls*   26

☆ *Sequence for Inbound Calls*   26

▶ LEARN TO LISTEN   27

▶ ACKNOWLEDGE   28

▶ MAKE A STATEMENT   30

▶ ASK A QUESTION   31

☆ *Open-Ended Questions*   32

☆ *Closed-Ended Questions*   33

☆ *Be Careful with Questions*   33

▶ CONSULTATIVE SELLING   35

Chapter IV   **SECRETS OF EFFECTIVE TELEMARKETING SCRIPTING**   **37**

▶ LISTENING: THE KEY TO GOOD COMMUNICATION   37

▶ NEVER DEFEND YOUR POSITION   39

▶ BE OBSERVANT OF PAUSES   39

▶ NERVOUS LAUGHTER CAN BE SERIOUS   39

▶ TREAT LITTLE PEOPLE BIG   40

▶ NEVER CALL WHEN ANGRY, SCARED OR DESPERATE   40

▶ AVOID BEING OVERLY FAMILIAR   40

▶ EVALUATE PERFORMANCE   41

▶ RESPONDING TO VOICE MAIL   41

▶ DEVELOP RAPPORT   43

▶ CHOOSE POSITIVE DESCRIPTIVE WORDS   44

☆ *Positive Descriptive Words*   45

Chapter V   **OUTBOUND CALLS**   **47**

▶ A COST-EFFECTIVE BUSINESS TOOL   47

▶ THE OPENER   48

☆ *The Greeting*   50

☆ *Identification*   50

☆ *Statement of Purpose*   50

☆ *Obtain Permission to Talk*   51

▶ WHEN IS PERMISSION NOT PERMISSION?   52

▶ ALTERNATIVES		53
▶ SURVEY CALLS		56
▶ SURVEY RULES		57
▶ QUALIFYING		59
▶ CONSULTATIVE SELLING		61
▶ THE OFFER		62
▶ HANDLING OBJECTIONS		63
▶ CLOSING		64
▶ THE WRAP-UP		66

Chapter VI   **INBOUND CALLS**   **67**

▶ GREETING THE CUSTOMER		70
☆ *Clear Identification*		70
▶ CONTROL THE CALL		70
▶ RESPONDING TO THE REQUEST		71
☆ *Identify the Prospect*		71
☆ *Determine the Prospect's Needs*		72
☆ *Providing a Sales Message and Asking a Question*		72
▶ CLOSING		73
☆ *Recommendations/Suggestions*		74
☆ *Ask for the Order*		74
☆ *Increasing or Upgrading the Order*		75
▶ WRAP-UP		75
☆ *Source the Call*		76
☆ *Summarize and Create Certainty*		76
▶ THE SIGN-OFF		76

Chapter VII   **ALL ABOUT OBJECTIONS**   **79**

▶ PRICE		81
▶ PRODUCT		84
▶ PROCRASTINATION		85
▶ PERSONALITY		87
▶ THE OBJECTION CYCLE		88

	❱ TSR OBJECTIONS	91
Chapter VIII	**SCRIPT FORMATTING AND ORGANIZATION**	**95**
	❱ BRANCHED SCRIPTS	97
Chapter IX	**SAMPLE SCRIPTS - OUTBOUND**	**107**
	❱ DIRECT SALES - OUTBOUND	107
	❱ OPENER	108
	❱ SAMPLE PROSPECT DEVELOPMENT SCRIPT - OUTBOUND	114
	❱ THINGS TO UNDERSTAND AND KNOW BEFORE YOU ATTEMPT TO USE THIS SCRIPT	114
	❱ SMITH & JONES PROSPECT DEVELOPMENT SCRIPT	115
	❱ SAMPLE INBOUND CUSTOMER SERVICE ORDER SCRIPT	119
	❱ INBOUND SCRIPT	119
Chapter X	**ASSESSING PERFORMANCE**	**123**
	❱ MONITORING AND COACHING	123
	☆ TSR/CSR MONITORING FORM	124
Chapter XI	**SOME FINAL ADVICE**	**125**
Chapter XII	**CODE OF ETHICS: DMA**	**127**
Appendix I	**SCRIPTWRITING FORMS**	**135**
	❱ TELEMARKETING DAILY PHONE LOG	139
	❱ DAILY TELEMARKETING CALL FORM	140
	❱ CALL MONITORING CHECK LIST	141
	❱ RESULTS OR REASONS	143
	❱ COMPETITIVE ADVANTAGE ANALYSIS	144
	TELEMARKETING RESOURCE GUIDE	**145**
	❱ ORDER FORM	151
	BIOGRAPHY: JUDY MCKEE	**153**
	BIOGRAPHY: NADJI TEHRANI	**154**

FOREWORD BY NADJI TEHRANI

Having been instrumental in bringing telemarketing to the forefront of acceptance in America and in most of the world with the 1982 introduction of *Telemarketing®* magazine, Technology Marketing Corporation is proud to bring you *SCRIPTWRITING FOR EFFECTIVE TELEMARKETING: The Guide to Successful Business by Phone.*

In our many years of industry leadership, we have repeatedly discovered that the difference between sales success and failure is often the quality of the script. To appreciate this point, consider these three descriptions of selling:

☎ Selling is the art of persuasion.

☎ Selling is the art of communicating benefits.

☎ Selling is the art of fulfilling customers' needs.

Whether the goal is to persuade, communicate or uncover customer needs, you must have an effective script. In selling, he or she who makes the most persuasive, professional, customer-oriented presentation gets the order.

We are all familiar with the "old school" of sales techniques that produced pushy, aggressive, hard-selling salespeople. Those techniques never worked, and they especially don't work in telephone sales. That is why this book, which significantly departs from tradition, represents a refreshing, new approach to selling. As Judy McKee says, it's a "kinder, gentler method of selling," which embodies the element of trust. Judy's philosophy is that *great scripts must incorporate fairness, integrity, honesty, dignity, service and quality.*

I couldn't agree with her more! These are the ingredients that generate customer trust. Without trust, no sales of any kind will take place. It is only common sense — You would never buy anything from someone you didn't trust. This is ten times more true in telephone selling, where buyers do not get to meet the TSRs (telephone sales representatives) or CSRs (customer service representatives) in person. Therefore, TSRs and CSRs must possess impeccable sales skills, and the message they impart from the script must be highly professional. In this pioneering book, Judy McKee will teach you how to achieve these results.

Judy has had a distinguished career in business and, more specifically, in what I call "sales diagnostics." Judy is no stranger to *Telemarketing*® magazine and Technology Marketing Corporation. She is a frequent author for *Telemarketing*®. She has also been a popular speaker at many of Technology Marketing Corporation's TBT® The Integrated Marketing Expo™ conventions, and has earned the respect of many sales and marketing executives over the years.

Her unique, "kinder, gentler" way of selling imparts professionalism and customer trust, which results in unprecedented sales. Although the slant of this book is on telephone selling, many of the ideas Judy presents can be equally applied to field sales or other sales communications.

In today's highly competitive business environment, you must prepare a masterful script to persuade customers to buy from you: this refreshing, new approach to scripting will help you do that. We urge you to read this informative book several times; analyze and digest it; and most important, apply it to all of your scripting requirements.

Sincerely,

Nadji Tehrani
President, Technology Marketing Corporation
Publisher, Telemarketing®*magazine*

ACKNOWLEDGMENT

I extend my sincere thanks to Judy McKee for preparing this excellent manuscript. I also sincerely appreciate the outstanding editing of this book by Linda Driscoll, editor of *Telemarketing*® magazine and vice president of Technology Marketing Corporation. In addition, I'm grateful for the careful copyediting of this book by Erik Lounsbury, assistant editor of *Telemarketing*® magazine and Sarah Rutledge, editorial coordinator of *Telemarketing*® magazine.

A very special appreciation is also extended to Lynn Jones for coordination, layout and production of this excellent work.

Nadji Tehrani
Publisher

INTRODUCTION

Every once in a while, a "natural" comes along. Naturals have a special charisma. A God-given talent. A rare ability. Naturals have extraordinary mental or physical attributes that enable them to make everything look easy. They can catch a fly ball, throw a strike, hit long, sweeping drives with little or no apparent effort. In business situations, they know what to say and how to say it. They can wing it in almost any circumstance and come out winners!

Unfortunately, we're not all like that. Most of us need training. We have to study, prepare and practice, practice, practice. When hiring telephone sales representatives (TSRs) or customer service representatives (CSRs), it's unusual to find a "natural."

We do the next best thing. We look for a person with good traits and abilities that can be molded into a form that will serve our purpose. We know that training and skill development are essential to obtain the kind of performance needed to successfully compete in today's fast-paced world.

Telephone mastery is a skill that can and must be developed in every person who will come in contact with business prospects, customers or clients. Well-written and well-executed telephone scripts can help ordinary people sound like "naturals."

You have probably heard the statement: "Plan your work and work your plan." Carpenters would not set out to build a house without a plan (some blueprints, a list of materials, a budget and a schedule for completion).

Using a detailed plan, carpenters can pursue their task with confidence and vision. They can measure their performance and minimize the surprises that can be encountered.

A written script for a telephone call can be likened to the carpenter's plan. The purpose of the script is to enable the TSR or CSR to maintain focus and control the conversation. It will guide the TSR or CSR to achieve the intended result of the call. Notice I did not say it should be used to control the *prospect*, but to control the path of the *call*.

Most of us have had experience with telemarketers' calls. Some of those experiences may have been good, but many others may have been bad.

Usually, in a "bad" call, the caller starts by saying: "How are you today?" (He or she is trying to develop a rapport, but is actually irritating you.) The caller doesn't really care how you are; usually he or she doesn't even wait for an answer. Then, the caller takes off on a seemingly unstoppable spiel about what he or she wants you to do — donate, buy, come in for a free widget, etc.

Most scripts are written to cram as many benefits as possible in the initial spiel, hoping that something that has been said will pique your interest enough so you will not slam down the phone.

This kind of telemarketing has given the industry a negative image and must be eliminated like the plague that it is. My mission is to stamp out the poor image of telemarketing. Therefore, I write scripts and train others to write scripts that are non-intrusive and non-manipulative. This "new age" script approach, although polite and considerate, is very effective in achieving the objectives of the call.

This book is about writing telemarketing scripts that will change the hard-sell approach to a kinder, gentler, more effective means of bringing valuable opportunities to consumers. By using this approach to scriptwriting, telemarketing sales representatives (TSRs) and customer service representatives (CSRs) will regain confidence and self-esteem, and find renewed pleasure in the important job of telemarketing.

The key to successful telephone scripting is "**The Statement/Question Technique**," which is the foundation of consultative selling. By using this technique, the TSR or CSR can engage the prospect or client in "designed dialog" that will lead the call to a successful conclusion without intimidation or manipulation. This skill gives the TSR or CSR total control over the call, which builds confidence and professionalism.

A simple way to gain a quick understanding of the difference between outmoded, traditional telemarketing scripts and the "new age" scripts is to compare the two methods.

The "Statement/Question Technique" should be thoroughly understood to attain the desired style and quality of the non-intrusive tone needed for successful telemarketing. I strongly recommend anyone who intends to write scripts to study and master "The Statement/Question Technique." It is thoroughly explained in Chapter III of this book. ☎

Judy McKee

TRADITIONAL SCRIPT	NEW AGE SCRIPT
Pitch	Consultative Dialog
Hard Sell	Kinder/Gentler Approach
Asks Intrusive/Assumptive Questions	Logical, Conversational Interview
Manipulates and Attempts to Control Prospect	Honestly Requests Permission, Showing Consideration and Respect
Never Asks a Question the Prospect Can Say "No" To	Always Asks Open-Ended Questions that Encourage the Prospect to Talk
"Overcomes" Objections	"Handles" Objections
Lacks Branching to Address Unforeseen Turns	Branching to Address Nearly All Possible Alternatives
Takes 15 Minutes to Write	Takes 4 to 10 Hours of Thoughtful Preparation
Intimidates TSRs and Causes Low Productivity	TSRs Feel Good About Using These Scripts
Low Success Rate	Higher Success Rate

CHAPTER I

THE TELEMARKETING INDUSTRY GROWS UP (But Not Without Pain)

Telemarketing is here to stay. According to *Telemarketing®* magazine, as well as Congressional findings that supported the Telephone Consumer Protection Act, more than 30,000 U.S. businesses were actively telemarketing goods and services to businesses and residential consumers.

It was estimated that more than 300,000 solicitors called about 18,000,000 Americans every day. The total U.S. sales generated through telemarketing amounted to $435 billion in 1990, a more than four-fold increase since 1984. And that amount is projected to double by the end of the century.

New and astonishing advances are being made every day in telecommunications technologies. To improve productivity, make more calls faster, and effectively manage data, today's telemarketer may use predictive dialing systems, automatic call distributors, automated management control systems, or any one of hundreds of other devices.

Despite technology's benefits, it is imperative that it does not obscure the need to develop and improve human skills, especially using the human voice to say the right words in the right way to potential customers.

Without proper skills and training in script use for CSRs, TSRs and managers, the rush to make more and more calls will degrade the quality and integrity of this powerful medium.

Telemarketing professionals cannot afford to allow the goose that lays the golden eggs to be killed. Be careful. The goose is in danger! Congress has passed the *Telephone Consumer Protection Act* to force legislation to control certain aspects of telephone sales that have gotten out of control.

The *Act* states, in part: "Individuals' privacy rights, public safety interests, and commercial freedom of speech and trade must be balanced in a way that protects the privacy of individuals and permits legitimate telemarketing practices."

Further, "Evidence compiled by Congress indicates residential telephone subscribers consider automated or pre-recorded telephone calls, regardless of content, to be a nuisance and an invasion of privacy." And finally, "many consumers are outraged over the proliferation of intrusive, nuisance calls to their homes from telemarketers."

Business operators who are greedy, insensitive or unscrupulous are giving telemarketing a poor image. They are literally poisoning the pool of potential customers through continued use of intrusive, manipulative or fraudulent techniques.

The Direct Marketing Association (DMA) has developed a *Code of Ethics* which can be found in Chapter XIII, which provides you with ethical guidelines to conduct a legitimate telemarketing operation.

In addition, I strongly urge all readers of this book, whether long-time telemarketers or beginners, to obtain a copy of the *Telephone Consumer Protection Act* from the DMA (address and phone number are printed at the end of Chapter XIII).

Please review these important documents and take all necessary steps to comply with the criteria set forth. This effort will ensure your immediate and long-term success, as well as preserve the rights of all who choose to use telemarketing as the privilege it is.

The scriptwriting techniques defined in the following chapters are based on a "kinder, gentler" approach to telemarketing that will be less intrusive and, in the final analysis, more acceptable to the public. ☎

CHAPTER II

PRE-SCRIPT PLANNING

MENTAL PREPARATION

The mental preparation of the scriptwriter can mean the difference between an ordinary script and a great one. Use a questionnaire format (see pages 21 and 22) to stimulate a flow of thoughts and ideas that become the framework of the script. You can use this form later as a checklist to ensure the final script addresses all the benefits and features you want to convey, as well as responses to obstacles/objections you may encounter.

DEFINITION OF PURPOSE

DEFINITION OF PURPOSE

A key element of script preparation is a clear, written *definition of purpose*. Do not confuse *purpose* in this context with goals or objectives. The purpose is the underlying reason for doing what you do. Some companies would call it their mission statement. Your purpose might be:

> **"To provide the highest possible quality products, on schedule, at the lowest possible prices."**

It might be:

"To build a broad-based clientele of satisfied customers through responsible telemarketing campaigns."

Clear definition of purpose is important, because if the scriptwriting task is approached with the underlying noble purpose in mind, the thought process will flow more readily and the words will sound sincere and accurate. This feeling is conveyed to the TSR who will use the script.

TSRs will be more effective if they feel they are providing a genuine service to the prospect instead of performing the role of an unwelcome intruder. I strongly recommend that you write down two or three purpose statements that are relevant to your call campaigns.

DEFINING THE OBJECTIVES

A well-written script should be designed to accomplish specific objectives. Write down the *primary* objectives you wish to accomplish with your call campaign.

Primary Objectives

Primary objectives usually fall into one or more of the following categories:

☎ Lead generation,

☎ Qualifying the prospect,

☎ Information gathering,

☎ Setting an appointment,

☎ Direct sales,

☎ Fund raising,

☎ Customer service,

☎ Relationship building.

Secondary Objectives

Also consider *secondary* objectives. A secondary objective is something you are willing to settle for if your primary objective cannot be met. For example: If your primary objectives are to qualify the prospect and set an appointment, but you are unable to reach the decision maker, a secondary objective would be to have the receptionist agree to a specific time and date for you to call back to reach the decision maker.

Or, suppose you have reached the decision maker, but he or she declines to set an in-person appointment. A secondary objective would be to create good will and have the prospect agree to accept a mailing explaining your products/services.

DEFINITION OF OBJECTIVES

It would be even better to obtain agreement for you to call back to discuss any service you may be able to provide after he or she has reviewed your mailing. Write down your primary and secondary objectives on your pre-scriptwriting planning sheet so you can be certain to include them in your script.

QUALIFYING THE PROSPECT

It's important to qualify the prospect at the outset of the call for several reasons. First, is to make certain the prospect is a current or potential user of your products or services, and to determine if the prospect fits your customer profile. This will save you time and money by not spending effort that will never yield any return.

Second, intelligently posed questions can enable you to find the potential customer's "hot button." This can guide you to a more successful sales approach. And finally, during the qualifying conversation, you can develop a pleasant rapport if you are careful not to appear intrusive or intimidating.

Once I drove 60 miles to meet with a prospective client only to find he couldn't make the decision. He was not the person responsible for hiring. Painfully, I realized I had not done a good job of qualifying the prospect, as I drove back to my office through two hours of heavy traffic.

Since I learned that lesson, I now simply ask a closed-ended question:

> "Is Ms. Johnson the person who will make the
> decision to hire me for the job? And, will she
> be at the meeting?"

Being faithful to this routine has saved me considerable time and frustration.

For your pre-call planning, prepare a list of questions you would like to ask the prospect that will determine qualification. Notice that some things you would like to know should not be asked directly, because the questions would be perceived as impertinent or none of your business. You may be able to obtain the information you want by asking the question in an oblique, veiled manner. For instance, if you need to know a company's approximate yearly sales volume, it usually won't work to ask:

"How much are your yearly sales?"

Decision makers are often reluctant to answer this question. A different way to obtain valuable information would be to ask:

"How many people do you employ?"

Obviously, a company that employs 10 people will generate less revenue than a company that employs 100 people. By knowing the number of employees, you can determine whether or not the prospect fits your customer profile with regard to size of operation.

Another touchy subject with decision makers concerns plans and budgets. If you ask the direct question,

"How much have you budgeted for computer purchases this year?"

you will most likely put the prospect on the defensive. A less intrusive question, but one that will give you a "feel" for potential possibilities, would be one that gives the prospect a choice, such as:

"Are you planning to add a large area network this year, or will you be staying with individual PCs?"

After you have listed the questions you would like to ask, carefully review each one and ask yourself, "Would I be willing to answer this question if a TSR was calling me?" If the answer is no, devise a way to veil the question so you get the information you want, without putting the prospect on the defensive.

Strive to limit your number of qualifying questions to the fewest possible that will provide the information you need. Remember, you are intruding on the prospect's time. Use the Statement/Question Technique (Chapter III) to make the survey as conversational as possible. "Open-ended" questions will encourage the prospect to talk. Write down the basic qualifying information you will need, and then phrase your questions in a way that is not intrusive or manipulative.

POTENTIAL OBSTACLES AND OBJECTIONS

Outbound telemarketing is intimidating to most people because they fear the uncertain aspects of calling a stranger who may reject them or make them feel foolish. The entire experience can be very frustrating because there are so many reasons for failure.

The cure for the fear of failure is preparing effective ways to deal with the obstacles and objections that may be encountered. Plan for all of the probable obstacles and objections and incorporate provisions to deal with these possibilities in your script. Examples of obstacles and objections are:

☎ Voice mail,

☎ Decision maker is not available,

☎ Decision maker has no time,

☎ Decision maker is loyal to an existing supplier,

☎ Decision maker is not interested,

☎ Procrastination,

☎ Price is too high,

☎ No budget,

☎ No need,

☎ Reasons peculiar to your particular product
 or service.

Statements and questions relevant to all of these above possibilities can be scripted so that the TSR can maintain control of the call and end up winning no matter what the outcome.

EXPECTED CHALLENGES

Write down what you feel will be the main challenges to successfully achieving your objectives. After you have written the initial draft of your script, use the list of challenges as a checklist to decide if your script is designed to truly achieve your objectives. Some major challenges would be:

☎ Getting to talk to the decision maker,

☎ Getting the decision maker to listen and respond to the sales message,

☎ Getting the decision maker to decide now.

COMPETITIVE ADVANTAGES AND BENEFITS

Successful businesses are always striving to establish and maintain competitive advantages. These are features of your company or your product that give you an edge. If you have a more convenient location than most of your competitors, lower pricing due to high volume or low overhead, and a 24-hour, on-call service department, you have competitive advantages that will benefit your customers.

List all of the reasons a prospective client could benefit from doing business with your company. This information will be used to compose effective sales message statements that provide compelling reasons for the prospect to be interested in what you have to say and ultimately to make a positive decision.

When I am writing scripts for clients, I always ask, "What's so great about you? Why should the customer do business with you instead of the competition? Tell me what you have to offer, and be sure it is specific and measurable by the people with whom you want to do business.

"Make sure it really matters to your prospect, and don't be afraid to put those wonderful things about your company right in the script, such as, 'We can provide an analysis of your business that will show you how to profit more, spend less and increase your sales by a minimum of 10 percent.' " Wow! ... Now you're talking.

DEFINE THE INITIAL OFFER

Notice in the script plan above, the company stated that it could help the client profit more and spend less. That was not all. It was specific and measurable about being able to increase sales by 10 percent or more. Don't be one of those companies that calls and says, "We will give you better service." State what you can do, and how you can prove it, but be ruthless in your integrity.

Defining the offer you will make to the prospect once you feel that he or she is interested in your products and/or services is very important. Offers can often be effectively stated in the form of a recommendation. For example:

Suppose your objective is to obtain an appointment with the decision maker to demonstrate a new plain-paper fax machine. Recommend that you drop by, bring the machine with you and show how the machine can save time and money right in his or her own office, in actual working conditions. Recommendations work well, especially if you have established yourself as an expert.

DEFINE THE FALL-BACK OFFER

A prospect may reject your initial offer, so be prepared to make a fall-back offer. The fall-back offer is important because it serves to keep the relationship open. The fall-back offer could be to provide a free inspection and tune-up of the prospect's copy machine by your factory-trained technicians. It's a good way to assess the customer's potential, start a friendly relationship, and show off your service capabilities.

**DEFINE
THE OFFER**

The fall-back offer may get you in the door when the initial offer fails.

CREATE A FORM

Make your planning task easier by having a form to complete. We are all accustomed to filling out forms. They serve as checklists to ensure that we are providing all of the required data. Create a form like the sample shown on pages 21 and 22. Make whatever changes or additions are needed to suit your particular business.

When you are satisfied that the form fits your circumstances, make at least 10 copies. Place them in a folder where you can easily access them when you are ready to write your next script. This form will be a valuable tool, and you will be glad you took the time to prepare it. ☎

SAMPLE PRE-SCRIPTWRITING PLANNING SHEET
❏ **OUTBOUND** ❏ **INBOUND**

1) Purpose of This Call Campaign
❏ To build a broad-based clientele of office products customers through responsible, but aggressive telemarketing.
❏ Make current and potential users aware of the significant savings and productivity gains available by using plain-paper fax machines.
❏ Make our client base aware of our revolutionary, new, 24-hour, on-call service policy.

2) Objectives of This Call Campaign
❏ Speak to the decision maker.
❏ Obtain an appointment to demonstrate equipment.
❏ Generate interest in receiving brochures and price lists and obtain permission to call back.

3) Qualifying Information Desired
❏ How many faxes sent/received daily?
❏ Are faxes copied and/or distributed?
❏ Are faxes filed for future action?
❏ What equipment is the prospect currently using?

4) Potential Obstacles and Objections
❏ Voice mail.
❏ Decision maker not available.
❏ Decision maker has no time to talk.
❏ No budget for new equipment.
❏ Client already has adequate fax machine.

PRE-SCRIPTWRITING PLANNING SHEET

5) Expected Challenges
- ❑ Getting to the decision maker.
- ❑ Getting decision maker to listen to sales message.
- ❑ Getting decision maker to act now.

6) Benefits and Features of Doing Business with Our Company
- ❑ Expert advice and guidance available — ensures customer gets exactly what he or she needs and wants.
- ❑ Available 24-hours, with on-call service and troubleshooting. Saves customer time and money with less downtime.
- ❑ Customer saves shopping time because we have a broad range of makes and models in one convenient showroom.

7) Competitive Advantages
- ❑ Pricing discounts due to volume of sales.
- ❑ Outstanding lease/purchase plan available.
- ❑ Conveniently located showroom and service department.

8) Define the Initial Offer
- ❑ Free consultation and in-office demonstration.
- ❑ Free inspection and tune-up of current machine.

9) Define the Back-Up Offer
- ❑ Send out brochures/flyers and obtain permission to call back.

CHAPTER III

THE STATEMENT/QUESTION TECHNIQUE: NEVER MAKE THE CLIENT FEEL WRONG OR STUPID

STATEMENT/ QUESTION TECHNIQUE

My motto has always been: "Never make the client feel wrong or stupid." It has long been my belief that people will do almost anything to be right. I was also one of those people. My early training in the old school of sales was the "get them before they get you" method. Intimidate and overcome the customer was the order of the day.

I detested that way of doing business, and found that I occasionally **won** in the short term, but nearly always **lost** in the long term. I knew several things about myself I thought should make me good at sales. I was a hard worker and really meant to truly serve my customers.

Although I was sure I was the best person for the job, I couldn't get many appointments using those outmoded methods. I tape-recorded all of my business calls and listened to myself for hours. The sudden realization was, **the person who asks the questions is in control.**

Also, it was apparent whenever I made a statement of acknowledgment ("yes, good, thank you, okay"), the customer felt I was actually listening, and we were having a **conversation**.

Another realization was when I agreed with customers, paraphrased what they said, made them *right* and *smart* instead of *wrong* and *stupid*, they continued to talk to me. So I made a list of statements and questions and worked them into my conversation. This has been my "No Hassle and No Hard-Sell Method" ever since.

I call it the "Statement/Question Technique." It's controlling the call, not the person being called. I make suggestions, recommendations and ask for the order without intimidating my customer or brow-beating my prospect. The happy result is many long-term associations and satisfied customers.

INITIATE A DIALOG

The Statement/Question Technique is a method of initiating dialog between the customer and the TSR or CSR that gives the TSR/CSR control of the call and, therefore, the confidence to make effective calls. It is a methodology I recommend you use throughout the script to help the TSR or CSR guide the conversation and achieve the objective.

The Statement/Question Technique will open up areas of conversation by using consultative questions. It will begin the process of pointing out features and benefits of your product or service that will solve the prospect's problems. **This is consultative selling.**

CONTROL THE CALL, NOT THE PROSPECT OR CUSTOMER

The TSR is always at the mercy of the prospect if the prospect asks the questions. A traditional technique used to handle this is to "answer a question with a question." When this technique is used, the customer feels manipulated and gets upset. The prospect does not feel as if the TSR is actually listening or trying to help. At this point, the TSR is at a disadvantage. Using the Statement/Question Technique, the TSR takes control and leads the prospective customer in the direction the TSR wishes to go.

TSR CONFIDENCE BUILDER

The TSR will gain confidence after putting this technique to work. The feeling of control and self-esteem that comes from knowing this skill builds confidence. As a result, the TSR will be more productive.

HOW IT WORKS

CONTROL THE CALL

The Statement/Question Technique has four parts. The parts are the same, but will be used in a different sequence depending on whether the call is **outbound or inbound.** As I describe the technique, I will speak directly to the TSR.

To be successful at calling, you must first be a good listener. Hear and visualize what the customer is saying. Let the person on the other end of the line know you hear and understand what is being said. Say something about what you heard and offer a solution or comment to satisfy the customer's request, and take control by asking a question.

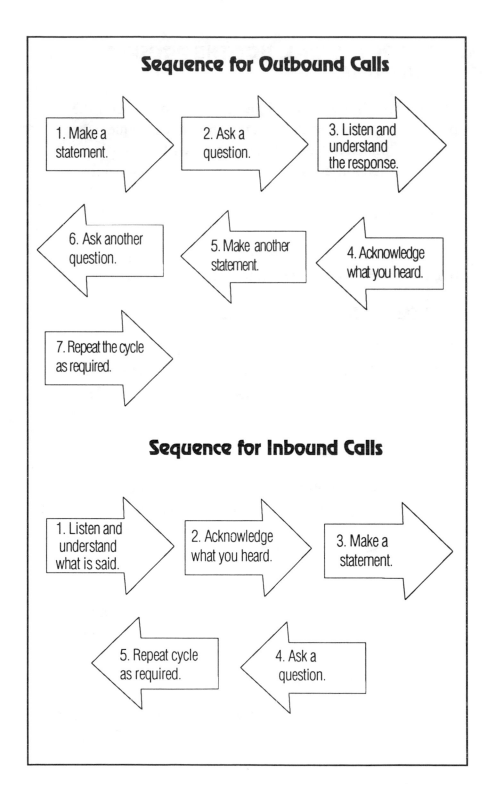

LEARN TO LISTEN

Pay close attention to what the customer is saying. Make a conscious effort to hear and understand what the customer means. To do this, you must recreate in your mind what you heard. See if you can picture the customer's situation. It is very important to develop the attributes of a good listener. Actually know what the customer *means*.

This was a lesson I learned very early on in the selling business. I was using the telephone to generate appointments in real estate sales. One day I called a woman about the possibility of listing her house. She told me she did not want to pay a commission to sell her home. I did not really listen to her. I was concerned about what I would say next, so, instead of *listening*, my mind was racing ahead to the next question.

I asked her if I could come by and see her house. She answered, "Aren't you listening ... I don't want to sell with a real estate agent and have to pay a commission."

SEQUENCE FOR OUTBOUND CALLS

By now, she was angry with me for not hearing what she had to say. She was worried about *money*. I did not succeed on that call, but in all calls after that, I started to seriously listen to what the prospect was saying.

The next time this happened to me, I was prepared with a statement that showed understanding and compassion for the prospect's situation. I was able to provide several convincing reasons why she needed my assistance, and we began to develop a friendly rapport. She invited me to come to her home for a free appraisal. Before the day was over, she had listed her home for sale with me.

The key was listening to her concerns. Actually, I was able to list and sell her home for a price that was more than she expected, even after paying a commission.

Have compassion for the prospect and develop the ability to understand the prospect's situation. Be able to convey your desire to help solve the problem with your services or product. Avoid placing judgment on what you hear. Just listen. Ask probing questions to gain complete understanding.

Have empathy, which is the ability to show that you can project yourself into the prospect's problem to better understand him or her. This helps you solve the problem the prospect has with your product or service.

 Remember how many times you were not heard or understood and how frustrated it made you feel.

ACKNOWLEDGE

It is necessary to acknowledge what you heard when attempting to generate true communication. The prospective customer needs to know he or she has been understood. To acknowledge what the customer has said, use words that are short or make a short sentence of acknowledgment. It demonstrates you are listening.

Instead of long, declarative sentences, use simple words and phrases, such as: great, fine, good, okay, I'm sorry to hear that, yes, I understand (nodding of the head does not work over the telephone). If the call is negative, use phrases like: I understand how you feel, yes, that is a bad situation, that's really sad that happened, we're sorry you had that bad experience.

These expressions of understanding and acknowledgment will let the customer know you heard what was said and, at the same time, that you are compassionate and can empathize with his or her position. However, in no way blame yourself or your company for the problem. You need to take responsibility for the problem, but not the blame. It is common to confuse responsibility and blame. Learn to understand the difference. It will save countless hours of grief, guilt and upsets.

I learned the difference between responsibility and blame in the '70s when I was taking a course in "higher consciousness." I wanted to become more aware of what life was all about. The best part of this course was learning what responsibility was and how to give up the feelings of guilt and blame. I once received a call from an irate customer who said I had sent him an invoice for a script that he not only didn't want, but didn't order. (Someone else in his company *did* order the script.)

The customer was probably having a bad day and reacted totally out of proportion to the size of the problem. Realizing he was irate, I took full responsibility for the event. It occurred in my world so I assumed responsibility, although I was not to blame.

I wanted to retain the customer, save the relationship and keep my integrity without guilt or blame. I told him to return the script and disregard the invoice. Then I said my records showed I had received an order from someone named "Marie." I told him I might have made a mistake in accepting an order from her and would be happy to take responsibility for the matter.

He called back within the hour and apologized. Marie had ordered the script and hadn't told him. He got to save face because Marie hadn't told him she ordered the script. I looked good because I was completely willing to fix the matter without placing blame on him or me.

Just by staying calm and taking responsibility, I was able to successfully defuse what could have been an ugly incident. Be willing to take responsibility and resist the temptation to "be right" or punish the other person for making a mistake.

Acknowledgment is the simplest part of the technique, but not always easy to do. Practice different ways of using this simple acknowledgment technique. Once you get in the habit of using it, you will find you are communicating much more effectively. The customer or prospect will always feel like he or she is being *heard.*

MAKE A STATEMENT

On inbound calls, start the call by making a statement that acknowledges what you have heard. This will show the customer you are listening, you care and are interested in him or her. Add a comment on what you have heard, which shows you understand the situation.

Next, convey a sales message by using short sentences about the company or the product to explain why the prospect should consider your solution. Statements can be used in selling the benefits of a product or service while handling the objections of the customer.

There are several possibilities at this point in the call. You can:

☎ Paraphrase what the customer has said,

☎ Answer the customer's questions,

☎ Handle an objection,

☎ Make a sales statement,

☎ Announce your intention,

☎ Explain a situation.

Write down the four most common things the prospective customer might say to you. Then make up a list of statements that addresses these comments.

ASK A QUESTION

You will learn to take control and guide the direction of the call using this final step of the technique. Every time you ask an appropriate question, it shows you are genuinely interested in the customer. This makes the call consultative in nature instead of the old "pitch and want" technique.

The person asking the questions is always in control of the call. When you ask questions, it allows you to steer the conversation. This works well whether the call is inbound or outbound. When you just make a statement without a question following it, the prospect has to make the next move. When you ask the question, you control the next part of the conversation.

When you ask questions, it gives you ownership of the call and helps you gain confidence and authority. In turn, it provides a greater opportunity for your success. The right questions move the conversation along. They allow you to guide the call in the direction of a close or a sale. It's very important to know and understand the different types of questions and when to use them.

Open-Ended Questions

Open-ended questions begin with what, how or why. They open dialog between you and the prospect, and keep the conversation going by encouraging the prospect to talk. To learn this thoroughly, practice writing questions relevant to your business that start with what, how and why. You will see that these types of questions lead to a two-sided dialog. Some examples are:

"What kind of business are you in, Mr. Brown?"

"How did you hear about us?"

"Why are you thinking of moving at this time, Miss Jones?"

Practice this technique verbally with a partner. It will demonstrate that this encourages the customer to talk freely. Responses to these questions will give you information that will be invaluable throughout the call when dealing with objections.

It is important to learn the difference between a question that is open (encouraging the customer to talk) and a question that is closed (the customer can answer with a simple yes, no or some other short phrase). When you ask a closed-ended question, you can immediately tell the difference.

Closed-Ended Questions

Closed-ended questions begin with words like will, does or can. These questions will usually yield only a simple answer. Generally, they are used to obtain feedback or qualifying information. They may also be used when setting appointments or in closing situations. Some examples are:

"Are you in the printing business?"

"Do you currently have a copy machine?"

"Did you receive the information we sent you?"

"Will you be in this afternoon?"

"Can you call back tomorrow?"

"Does your company plan to expand in the field of telemarketing?"

"Shall we send that order out today?"

**OPEN- &
CLOSED-ENDED
QUESTIONS**

Be Careful with Questions

Watch out for questions that are too direct and intrusive. Nuances are *very important*. Make sure you check the buying temperature after each question during your practice periods. If a question seems to upset your role-playing customer, it will probably upset the customer in real situations as well. Rephrase your questions so they are not intrusive.

Here are some examples of questions I think are too direct. The prospect may feel the answers to questions like these are none of your business, and will become irritated.

"Do you have a budget for a new computer this year?"

"Can you tell me how much you are planning to spend for a speaker?"

"Do you have a strategy for increasing your business this year?"

"What problems are you having now?"

"How much time do you plan to spend on that item?"

Try to phrase these questions in a less intrusive manner. For example:

"If you put in a new computer, Mr. Jones, approximately how much do you think you would need to spend to get what you want?"

"Speaker fees can vary a great deal. What did you have in mind?"

"Strategies can be very helpful. What kinds of marketing plans are you thinking about?"

"We have solutions to many of the situations our clients are experiencing. How could we be of help to you?"

"About that proposal, do you think it will take two days or maybe more like a week to finish it? (Multiple choice makes it safer for the prospect to answer.)

CONSULTATIVE SELLING

The secret of consultative selling is to be **customer driven** and learn to listen to and solve the needs of the customer. The result of effective consultative selling is to be perceived as a problem solver and develop a warm, enduring relationship with your customer.

By understanding the Statement/Question Technique and consultative selling, you, the manager, will be prepared to write a script that will cover almost every situation. It will enable you to expect the unexpected, help the customer get what he or she wants and needs, and most important, guide the customer to accept the TSR as an **expert — a welcome resource. ☎**

CONSULTATIVE SELLING

CHAPTER IV

SECRETS OF EFFECTIVE TELEMARKETING SCRIPTING

Long ago, I learned that you can save valuable time and avoid frustration if you concentrate on what works and pay attention to the nuances of the calls you make or receive. I use these nuances as a guide to constantly revise, update or improve my scripts and training.

It is difficult to incorporate all the nuances into a script. After all, a script, no matter how comprehensive, is still just a guide. When there is a "live" person on the line, there is no sure way of telling where the conversation may lead, even though you use the Statement/Question Technique (see Chapter III) to maintain control.

LISTENING

When you are planning your scriptwriting, or training your TSRs or CSRs, be sure to incorporate the following concepts and techniques.

LISTENING: THE KEY TO GOOD COMMUNICATION

Listen carefully to what the prospect or customer is saying. Notice reactions to what you say. Try to understand what each person's reaction means. It will be necessary for you to take some action or make some response based on what the prospect meant, not necessarily on what he or she said.

Have you ever had a conversation with someone you were sure wasn't listening while you were talking? Did the person seem to be thinking about what he or she was going to say when you stopped? I've noticed that many people don't give a direct answer to the actual question asked. For example, I overheard part of the following conversation:

> Mary: George, how far is it to Phoenix?
>
> George: I'm sure it's cheaper by bus.
>
> Mary: Mother said we had to be sure to be there by dinner time, so we'll have to leave no later than noon, won't we?
>
> George: Well, we certainly can't afford to fly over there all the time.

This couple, although they seemed to communicate in some way, certainly lacked a lot in their listening and communication skills. Her focus was on getting to Phoenix in time for dinner. His focus was on how much it was going to cost to get there.

It's very difficult to be successful in telemarketing unless you get the prospect's attention on your intention. Getting the prospect to stay focused on your intentions is crucial to your success.

Learn to recognize customers' messages. For example, if the customer seems focused on cost, turn to the portion of your script where you deal with cost or price objections. There is no use in continuing your presentation until you have *handled* this objection.

NEVER DEFEND YOUR POSITION

If the customer or prospect is upset, you must try to feel what the customer is feeling. To eliminate or diminish the problem, let the person know you understand how he or she feels, without taking blame.

If you resist, or defend your position, it will make the person feel you are trying to be right, and make him or her wrong. It is better to show understanding, because the problem will then begin to dissolve. It doesn't work to resist what the other person is saying.

BE OBSERVANT OF PAUSES

Pauses usually mean the prospect or customer does not agree with what you have said. This often happens after you have made a statement that was meant as a sales message, such as, "Our product is the finest widget available today." Says who? You?

No matter what the reason for the pause, the TSR needs to determine what it means. Any break in communication must be mended before meaningful dialog can continue. It's important to be very conscious of the nuances moment by moment. My advice is don't rush ... go slowly ... handle all of the objections. The call will turn out better if you do.

NERVOUS LAUGHTER CAN BE SERIOUS

Inappropriate laughter (or comments) often indicates something you said has created a threatening or uncomfortable situation for the prospect. It may mean the prospect feels the answer to a direct question you asked is none of your business.

For example, I have seen scripts that ask, "How much do you plan to spend on computer hardware this year?" The answer is nearly always vague, and may cause the prospect to decide to terminate the conversation, which had been going well up to that point. It may be too late to recover on that particular call, but serious consideration should be given to deleting that question or rephrasing it in a less direct way for future calls.

TREAT LITTLE PEOPLE BIG

Secretaries, receptionists or any call screener should be treated with great respect. Although they usually don't make the decisions to buy or grant an appointment, they can impede your progress in reaching the decision maker. Treat everyone with kindness and respect.

Make call screeners feel they are very important, and you will have a better chance to get to Mr. or Ms. Decision Maker. Be sure your script is written to convey this feeling, and train your TSRs to use a tone and attitude that will convey the feeling as well.

NEVER CALL WHEN ANGRY, SCARED OR DESPERATE

Be certain callers are in a clear state of mind and are focused on the job at hand. No matter how good the script, poor attitude and tone are easily conveyed to the prospect or customer.

AVOID BEING OVERLY FAMILIAR

People in business have too much to do to spend time talking with you for the fun of it. When calling someone you don't know, don't ask, "How are you today?" Don't expect them to tell you they are having a miserable day or that Aunt Ida died last night and they are upset. Asking a stranger "How are you?" is an intrusion. The unspoken response or thought is, "It's none of your business ... what do you want?"

This automatically puts you, the caller, at a disadvantage. It's better to politely state who you are, why you are calling, and ask, "Do you have a moment to talk?" It's all right to ask, "How are you?" if you already have an acquaintance with the person you are calling, but please avoid it with strangers.

EVALUATE PERFORMANCE

If you are the one making calls, evaluate your own performance. Record several calls each week and listen to how you sound. Listen for the nuances. If you have TSRs making calls, arrange to regularly monitor calls so you can detect any possible flaws in the script or its delivery.

EVALUATE
PERFORMANCE

Developing an effective script is an iterative process. Scripts need to be updated with new offers and as products change or services grow. I'm not suggesting that you try to fix it if it's working well. Just be aware that there is always room for improvement. In my own business, at the end of each day, I note and write down what could have made the script more effective. This is the path to perfection.

RESPONDING TO VOICE MAIL

Voice mail can be very frustrating if you are trying to reach a decision maker. It's the ultimate call screener when it comes to obtaining an appointment, gathering survey intelligence, or making a sales presentation. If the decision maker doesn't *want* to talk to you, he or she just won't call back.

When you reach voice mail, you have two choices. The first is to simply hang up and try again later when the voice mail or answering machine may not be engaged. The second choice is to leave a well-scripted message that may be compelling enough to entice the decision maker to call you. I suggest the latter choice.

Since you have spent the money and time to make the call and have reached a machine, you might as well go through with it and give it your best shot. One of my clients at a major corporation claims he has had very good success (relatively speaking) at getting voice mail call backs by using the following script:

> "Hi, this is Tom Holt with XYZ Corporation. We have developed some new technology in conjunction with one of our business partners that you may find to be a real breakthrough timesaver for your medical accounts billing procedure. If you would care to chat about it, I can be reached at 800-XXX-XXXX. If this sounds like something you would be interested in, we have a full, descriptive, free pamphlet telling how it works. Once again, that number is 800-XXX-XXXX. My name is Tom Holt. Thanks."

Notice this message is non-intrusive, non-manipulative and straightforward. It states the benefit for the person being called, a possible solution, a breakthrough timesaver. It invites the prospect to "chat." This is a very non-threatening invitation, and it offers a **free,** descriptive pamphlet that can be obtained by calling an 800 number.

If the person being called gets the feeling that he or she can benefit from this new technology, this message conveys the feeling that they have nothing to lose by learning more. Try using this approach with voice mail. What do you have to lose?

DEVELOP RAPPORT

Rapport, loosely defined, means having something in common; a relationship. When we have rapport with others, it's easier to converse. It feels like we are friends. There are many techniques for developing rapport, including:

☎ Using the other person's name in the conversation, especially when asking a direct question and when mentioning money or time required for an appointment.

☎ Mentioning common acquaintances by name, if you have any.

☎ Asking questions that show you are truly interested in what the prospect has to say or the way he or she feels about a situation. **The best way to be an interesting person is to show you are interested in the person with whom you are talking**. Be careful to frame questions so you don't appear to be nosy.

☎ Acknowledge that you heard what the other person said. Let him or her know you are listening and understand what is being said. Do this by listening carefully and then paraphrasing what you heard. Paraphrase it in a way that's reflective of how the prospect said it.

Obviously, this cannot be scripted, but with training, it can become a skill TSRs can use effectively. If the prospect speaks loudly or softly, quickly or slowly, adopt that trait in your feedback and in the full course of the conversation. Someone who speaks slowly and softly may be put off by your speech if it is very loud and rapid. To be a truly successful communicator, be willing and capable of adapting your pace and style to match the other speaker.

CHOOSE POSITIVE DESCRIPTIVE WORDS

Scripts that contain positive descriptive words and phrases are much more likely to be successful. You will be taken more seriously if you are perceived as a "get things done" type who has definite answers and knows where he or she is going. Also, descriptive words and phrases, when properly strung together, can create a picture to which the prospect can relate.

Creating a picture will tend to increase the prospect's inclination to believe what you say. For example, instead of saying "A plain-paper fax machine will save you time," you should say, "A plain-paper fax machine gives you a copy that's immediately ready to go to work, with no curling up and no need to make a copy you can write on."

Following is an example of some useful descriptive words. I'm sure you can think of many more. Make a list of the ones you like best and consciously weave them into your scripts. ☎

Positive Descriptive Words

Admired	Free	Mannered	Quality
Aggressive	Friendly	Marketable	Rare
Amusing	Frugal	Mature	Recommend
Attractive	Full	Measurable	Relief
Bargain	Further	Motivating	Rewarding
Beautiful	Gentle	Much-needed	Safe
Beneficial	Genuine	Natural	Secure
Benefits	Gift	Necessary	Sociable
Capable	Give	Never	Stable
Cash	Guaranteed	New	Stimulating
Challenging	Guide	Now	Strong
Classic	Happy	Non-intrusive	Sympathetic
Cooperative	Healthy	Non-manipulative	Tailored
Creative	Hospitable	Opportune	Talented
Dedicated	Immediately	Outgoing	Tasteful
Diversified	Independent	Outstanding	Unique
Dynamic	Informative	Plush	Up-to-date
Efficient	Innovative	Pleasant	Upgraded
Elegant	Instantaneous	Popular	Urgent
Exactly	Integrity	Powerful	Valuable
Extraordinary	Leading edge	Prime	Value-added
Fantastic	Lucrative	Problem-solving	Variable
Fast-paced	Luxurious	Progressive	Vital
Formidable	Major	Quick	Youthful

**POSITIVE
DESCRIPTIVE
WORDS**

CHAPTER V

OUTBOUND CALLS

A COST-EFFECTIVE BUSINESS TOOL

Outbound telemarketing is a cost-effective way to introduce your company, products and services to new clients. It can help secure a steady new supply of business you need for growth.

Also, it's just plain profitable to call existing customers to inform them of special promotions, remind them of minimum inventory values they are maintaining (it's time to reorder), and other aspects of account management, showing you have their interest at heart and are intent on retaining their business.

Sales lead qualification is designed to reduce the number of wasted in-person sales visits. The costs of in-person industrial sales calls has now escalated to the point where most companies cannot afford to send salespeople to call on unqualified prospects. When a prospect is pre-qualified by telephone, telemarketing helps direct outside salespeople where the highest sales potential exists.

"Balloons Are Everywhere," a national marketer of party favors and floral supplies, uses telemarketing as a complete account management tool in conjunction with a splendid and frequently updated catalog. This allows the company to capitalize on the revenue potential of smaller accounts without the high cost of face-to-face sales visits. Outbound calling to a large number of small accounts that are spread over a wide geographic area permits profitable coverage at low cost.

The company's full-service telemarketing operation includes both selling and customer service. It involves order taking, answering questions about order status, inventory availability, shipment scheduling and billing, credit checking and product consultation.

The potential for using telemarketing is as broad as the imagination. The trick is putting together a comprehensive plan driven by a powerful script that will enable the user to realize the maximum gain from every opportunity.

The "raw material" for the script is gathered using the pre-scriptwriting planning form that was discussed in detail in Chapter II. Assuming the pre-scriptwriting planning form has been filled out and you are clear about your purpose and objectives, let's proceed to the first building block of an outbound script.

THE OPENER

An effective opening statement is the single most important part of the call. If you don't get past the opening, no objectives will be reached. Prospective clients make big decisions about you, your company and possibly your product just by hearing your voice on the opening of a call. The situation gets even more sticky when you consider the person you are calling is probably busy, doesn't like sales calls, and may have no immediate need for the opportunity you are trying to present.

You have about 20 seconds from the start of the call to create a "love me — trust me" feeling with the prospect where he or she feels safe and makes a decision about talking with you or turning you away.

The aim is to create an atmosphere that is conducive to open discussion. Make sure the prospect does not feel threatened or in danger of being conned, manipulated or otherwise put-upon. The opening can generate a strong feeling of resentment or a feeling of "everything is okay." Naturally, you want the prospect to feel comfortable and open.

THE OPENER

Some of this feeling can be conveyed by spoken words and can, therefore, be written in the script. But a large portion of the feeling comes from **how the words are said**. Although that can't be scripted, with a little practice and coaching, most TSRs can quickly learn what sounds sincere and non-manipulative.

The TSR must sound pleasing and appropriately energetic, i.e., be as light-hearted and full of enthusiasm as the product or service dictates.

The opener has four distinct parts: the greeting; identification; statement of purpose; and obtain permission to talk.

The Greeting

The greeting is very simple — "good morning," "good afternoon," "good evening," or just plain "hello."

Identification

Next comes the identification. This must clearly state the name of the TSR and the company he or she represents. Proper identification at the outset of the call is now required by federal and state laws.

Statement of Purpose

The third part of the opener, and the one that takes the most thought, where you make it or break it, is the statement of purpose, which informs the prospect why you are calling.

The statement must arouse the prospect's interest, giving him or her a reason to listen. Make use of **words that sell**, such as: new, innovative, exciting, delicious, rare and any other visual or sensual, stimulating adjectives that create a mental image while describing your product or service (see Chapter IV for a list of positive, descriptive words). Look at this example:

> "Good morning, Mr. Jones. My name is Georgia Smith with Radio Station KLSX. We have a very exciting promotion starting next week that's especially for new businesses like yours. Do you have a moment to talk?"

This opening follows the formula exactly. This opening statement should definitely arouse the interest of the person being called. If Mr. Jones has a new business, he will want to hear what Ms. Smith has to offer. If she was calling an established business, she would leave out the word "new."

Obtain Permission to Talk

The fourth and last part of the opener is the request for permission to talk. Always obtain permission to talk to the prospect at the opening of the call. It is an acknowledgment that you may be intruding, or that you may have caught him or her at a bad time. It's a subtle way of saying "I'd like to have your full attention and I'm willing to wait or call back later because I'm serious!"

Most of all, it shows that you are a polite person and that you have manners. How refreshing — especially in a world where pushy, tricky, manipulative people are clamoring for your attention.

STATEMENT OF PURPOSE

During a seminar I recently gave at a national telemarketing conference, I suggested to the audience that they ask for permission to speak when they got the decision maker on the line. Several people raised their hands and said they were taught that they should never ask the prospective customer a question that could be answered with "no." I replied that I thought that was "old-fashioned selling."

It is time to realize that the public is not stupid and, in fact, is over-informed. It is time to be polite and ask for permission. This gives prospects the chance to say "no," but they are saying "no" because they do not have time, not as a rejection of the caller.

There was still some rumbling in the audience about giving the prospect a chance to get away so soon in the conversation. Just then, one of the people in the seminar, a vice president of a major corporation, asked to tell his story. He said his company really believed in scripting and had changed only one thing in its script last year. They asked for permission. Their results went from $6 million in sales to $9 million that year.

He is not sure if the increase can be attributed to the permission question, but his TSRs feel they are being more polite, have the attention of the prospect and results have vastly improved.

WHEN IS PERMISSION *NOT* PERMISSION?

There are times when what you thought was permission was not really permission. Examples include prospects with the "giving in" attitude who say, "Yeah, go ahead, shoot," meaning hurry up, be quick and let's get this over with; or, "Okay, what do you want to sell me?"

Real permission is critical to your success, so there is no point in going on without it. I recommend you ask for permission again, and use the Statement/Question Technique. The tone of voice used here must be absolutely without guile or sarcasm. Example:

The prospect says, "Okay, go ahead." The TSR should say, "Mr. Smith, it sounds like I may have caught you at a bad time. Would it be better if I called you back later? Would that work better for you?"

This is a double question and makes your request seem very polite and sincere.

Or, if the prospect says, "Sure, but be quick about it. I don't have much time," the TSR can regain control of the conversation by saying, "It sounds like you are very busy right now, Mr. Jones. This exciting, new promotional opportunity may take a couple of minutes to properly explain. Should I call back later, or would you have just a couple of minutes now?"

This response gives the prospect a choice. He or she can elect to wait to hear the offer or do it now. Listen for a change in tone from the prospect. If he or she chooses to do it now, it will be in a more relaxed, receptive manner. If the choice is to call back, the TSR now has a valid telephone appointment. This attitude will be appreciated, and the TSR will be remembered as a unique telemarketer.

ALTERNATIVES

Here is a valuable tip about alternatives: the alternative you want the prospect to choose should be stated last. Most people have a tendency to be lazy about choices, and unless they really think about it, will usually choose the last alternative they hear. **Put the choice *you* want last.**

Following are samples of different kinds of openers for your review. Some variation of these will probably be a good opener for your first masterful script.

Sample Sales Openers:

☎ *Greeting.*

☎ *Identify yourself.*

☎ *Ask for the prospect.*

1) "Good morning. My name is Lisa with Credit Card Services. May I please speak to Mr. Green?"

You have reached the prospect. Go to #2a.

2a) "Oh good, Mr. Green. I am calling from 1-800-YOURCARD to tell you that because of your excellent credit rating, you have been prc-approved for a credit card. Do you have a moment to talk?"

Or ...

2b) "Good morning, Mr.Green. My name is Lisa. I'm calling from the New and Blue office in Minnesota. We have some good news for those people who have reached the qualifying age for Medicare health coverage. Do you have a moment to talk?"

The prospect says yes. Go to #3.

3) "Good! The good news is that **new** Medicare enrollees aged 65 and older will have six months in which to obtain supplemental health insurance **without fear of rejection or having to meet medical underwriting requirements**. Are you planning to apply for Medicare coverage, Mr. Green?"

Opener for a response to a bingo card or a request for information where the prospect has shown an interest in some way:

☎ *Greeting.*

☎ *Identification.*

☎ *Announce that he/she requested this information.*

☎ *Ask permission to ask some questions first, qualifying the prospect.*

☎ *Ask about six questions and NO more.*

"Good afternoon. My name is John with Skills Diagnostics. May I please speak to Mrs. Hanson? Mrs. Hanson, my name is John with Skills Diagnostics and we received a request from you for some information about our new DIGITAL-SKILL-ALERT System, but to ensure we send the information that is relevant to your operation, we need to ask you a couple of questions. Do you have a minute to talk?"

Yes.

"Great! Mrs. Hanson, are you the person responsible for the Training Department at your company?"

(If not, obtain the name of the correct person.)
(If yes, proceed to ask the survey questions.)

Opener for a follow-up call to information that has been sent at the request of the prospect:

☎ *Greeting.*

☎ *Identification.*

☎ *A statement regarding what was sent.*

☎ *Ask to be connected directly to the prospect.*

Receptionist answers ...

"Good morning, this is Joshua with *Acme Construction News*. We sent Mr. Smith a sample copy of our publication for his review. I promised to call back to discuss any questions or comments he may have. Please connect me with Mr. Smith."

You have reached the prospect ...

"Good morning, Mr. Smith. This is Joshua with Publishers Company. We sent you a sample copy of the *Acme Construction News* for your review. Do you have a moment to talk?"

SURVEY CALLS

Survey calls can be very valuable. A market-driven company can determine which products sell best, why their customers like one style, but not another, and so on. Survey calls must have carefully written scripts, and must avoid taking up too much of the customer's time.

Simple information-gathering surveys that don't include a sales pitch or require no follow-up should offer the customers an incentive to stop whatever they are doing and answer the survey questions. Coupons for the product or a free sample to come in the mail are appropriate incentives.

It is totally unacceptable, however, to use the survey as a ploy to reach an underlying sales or appointment-setting goal. The only acceptable alternative is to tell the consumer up front what is going to happen and get permission to do it. Then there will be no problem later in the call. The TSR will not sound "manipulative" when asking for an order or an appointment.

I have noticed that TSRs and CSRs who are asked to be "tricky" or feel they are being manipulative have poor results. The truth must be told in the opening of the call. This usually alleviates the uncomfortable feeling. The prospect will be informed and will have given permission for whatever is going to happen. This works!

SURVEY RULES

☎ Announce the amount of time it will take to complete the survey.

☎ No survey should contain more than 20 questions.

☎ Questions should be easy and short, requiring brief answers.

☎ Use only one essay question per survey, i.e., "Tell me in your own words why you really like to use Always Ready Batteries in your child's toys."

☎ Offer an incentive or a reward for using the consumer's time.

☎ Tell the consumer what you intend to accomplish with the survey and how it will be of benefit in the long run.

☎ Thank the consumer and state when the gift can be expected.

☎ Hang up last — after the consumer.

Suggested openers for surveys requiring no selling or requests for appointments:

☎ "Good evening, Mr. Erickson. My name is Sarah with Consumer Plus. We are the company that surveys customers for our clients to see how they can better serve you, the consumer. We will send you a wonderful coupon booklet worth $30 if you will give us about five minutes to answer these questions. Okay?"

☎ "Good evening, Mr. Erickson. My name is Sarah with Teleflex Services. We are calling all of our customers who have joined us in the last six months just to be sure they are receiving the best possible service from us. Do you have a couple of minutes to answer about six questions?"

☎ "Hello, Mr. Erickson. My name is Sarah with POPS Up Popcorn Company. We have a gift to send you if you will answer some of our questions about how you prepare and serve our product. Do you have a couple of minutes?"

☎ "Good evening, Mr. Erickson. My name is Sarah with ABC Cosmetics. We are a market-driven company and want to determine if our customers are using our products as recommended. We are taking a survey and offering some specials and gifts today to the people who are willing to assist us in our marketing efforts. Do you have a minute?"

Suggested openers for a survey with appointment request:

☎ "Good morning, Ms. Wilcox. My name is Kevin with IMB Corporation, and we have a new software product that you may find very helpful in your type of business. We will send you a free demo diskette of this software if you will answer a few questions for us. If you like, we can even send a business representative to give you more information later. Do you have a couple of minutes to talk?"

☎ "Good morning, Ms. Wilcox. My name is Kevin with Lane Advertising. We have a gift for all of our customers who answer our survey questions, and we also offer to have a business representative come to your place of business, if you wish, to show you how our advertising works. There are six questions. Do you have a couple of minutes?"

Suggested opener for a survey with a sales pitch at the end:

☎ "Hello, Ms. Wilcox. My name is Kevin with Marquee Health Insurance Company. We are taking a survey of the people in St. Louis who may need an extra medical supplement to Medicare. Would you mind answering a few questions? We can make you a special offer at the end of this survey call. Would that be okay with you?"

QUALIFYING

The process of qualifying prospects can be made much less intrusive if done in a conversational manner. You can incorporate qualification inquiries in the "statement of purpose" portion of the call. Use the Statement/Question Technique to state your purpose, and, at the same time, determine if your prospect is a potential customer for your product or service.

Let's suppose you're prospecting for clients for your home maintenance and repair service. You might be tempted to ask direct questions, such as:

"Do you own or rent?" and, "How old is your home?"

I suggest you try this kinder, gentler approach instead:

"We are calling homeowners to introduce our new home maintenance policy with an initial free termite inspection. Mr. Jones, how long have you been living in your present home?"

In this scenario, your most qualified prospect would own his or her own home and have lived in it for five years or more. In the suggested approach, you have not directly asked the prospect if he or she owns or rents. The statement assumes the prospect is a homeowner.

If the prospect is not the homeowner, he or she will most certainly express disinterest and say he or she is a renter. You have obtained the information you need, but in a conversational way. If the prospect is a homeowner, you can continue your sales message by further explaining the features and benefits of your service.

Take care not to let your qualifying sound like an inquisition. Try to phrase your statements and questions in a manner that will convey an impression of "love me, trust me."

Prospects often feel they are being set up if they don't know why you're asking the questions. When asking qualifying or survey questions, it's best to first explain the purpose and benefits for the prospect.

When writing a script, imagine yourself in the prospect's situation and ask yourself if you would be comfortable responding. If your answer is no, rewrite the statements and questions in a less threatening way.

CONSULTATIVE SELLING

Reputable doctors usually don't prescribe a remedy until they have diagnosed the ailment. Reputable salespeople can save themselves and the prospect much wasted time and effort if they target their presentation to the prospect's needs.

Once you have gotten into a relationship with the prospect, you assume the doctor role, asking, in effect, "What is your problem, where does it hurt, how does it feel?" Answers to appropriate questions will give you valuable insight into the areas where your prospect will be responsive.

When you increase your knowledge of his or her situation, you can make meaningful recommendations to solve problems with your product or service. This is the way to become perceived as a resource instead of a nuisance. The key is to be able to phrase probing questions in a manner that will not be construed as "nosy."

Your phrasing of the questions should convey genuine interest that indicates you are trying to help rather than trying to sell something. Put the focus on the prospect and his or her situation, not on you and your sales objective. A good assessment of the prospect's situation provides a logical opening where you can state the benefits of your products and/or services. Strive to make this consultation as conversational as possible.

Follow these simple rules for success:

1. Use open-ended questions whenever possible. These questions begin with what, how, when or where. Open-ended questions encourage the prospect to talk.

2. Acknowledge what you hear with simple words or phrases, or with additional questions that will further draw out the prospect.

3. Make certain your following statements and/or questions maintain the path of the established conversation. Stay on the subject of the problem at hand.

4. Make recommendations and suggestions that provide solutions to the stated problems.

5. Strive to be perceived as an expert equipped with desirable resources the prospect can use to his or her advantage.

THE OFFER

After you have determined the prospect is qualified, it is appropriate to proceed with your primary offer. It should be stated clearly and simply so the prospect doesn't have to "sort out" your message. Long, complicated pitches can be confusing and cause the prospect to become disinterested. An example of the offer is:

> "Ms. Falworth, we are featuring free installation for all new cable service subscribers this month. Our package is only $29.95 per month, it provides 24-hour per day programming, and it includes both movie channels. Would you like to order that today?"

If the prospect declines your initial offer, be prepared with a secondary offer. It's best not to have too many choices, which can create confusion. Stay with one offer at a time. An example of a secondary offer would be:

> "Ms. Falworth, I understand that you don't care for the movie channels. Our basic service, which includes all major network programming, is only $18.95 per month, and you still get the free installation if you sign up now. Would that work better for you?"

Notice that both the primary and secondary offers state features or benefits of the service and that installation is free if the prospect acts now. When writing the offer portion of the script, try to relate the appealing features and benefits of your products or services in a simple, straightforward manner, and provide an incentive to act now.

HANDLING OBJECTIONS

Objections are often veiled requests for additional information or more logic on why the customer should buy your product or service. Some sales trainers use the term "overcome objections." I prefer the term "handle the objections." I do not believe that prospects wish to be overcome, bullied or manipulated into making a decision.

HANDLING OBJECTIONS

I believe that honest consultation and logical reasoning will far better serve the prospective customer.

Generating a feeling of trust and showing that you genuinely have the customer's interest at heart will serve you better in the long term. Objections are handled by paraphrasing what the prospect said, making a sales statement relevant to the objection, and then asking another closing question or making another closing recommendation. (See Chapter VII — "All About Objections.")

CLOSING

Closing is a logical conclusion to an effective presentation. The intent is to help the customer make a decision to buy, grant an appointment, come into the store or agree to whatever your primary or secondary objective may be. It's usually done at or near the end of your presentation when you feel you have met your prospect's needs.

Closing is most effective immediately after answering a question or handling an objection. Questions from the prospect near the end of your presentation are almost always "buying questions." I recommend answering the "buying questions" and then asking the closing question.

In Chapter VII, "All About Objections," I discuss the "sales cycle," where the prospect poses an objection, the TSR "handles" the objection and asks the closing question. This cycle may be repeated many times during the call, but persistence is the key. If you have done a good job planning for obstacles and objections, you should have a response ready for almost any situation that arises.

If you have been successful in maintaining the prospect's interest up to this stage, he or she will be expecting to hear a final closing question. Many salespeople are afraid to ask for the order because they feel this is the time when they may fail. The prospect may say no and all their effort will be lost.

This condition often causes TSRs to become uneasy. Their lack of confidence is transmitted to the prospect through their tone or hesitant actions. This can be overcome with practice and adopting the attitude that the prospect wants to be helped to make a buying decision.

Final closes can be done in the form of a simple question, such as:

"Would you like to take advantage of this free trial offer?"

Or, a final close can be phrased in the form of an assumption, such as:

"Our installer can put in your system right away. Would this afternoon or tomorrow morning be better for you?"

The latter example assumes the prospect is convinced to accept the offer and provides him or her with a choice of when the action should occur. It is effective and often used, but unless the TSR has developed a good rapport, it can be irritating or threatening to the prospect.

Don't be afraid to ask for the order. Simply ask in a non-threatening way after you think the customer feels good about your relationship. The prospect *expects* you to ask for the order; and rest assured, your sales-to-call ratio will be very poor if you don't.

Your script should have at least two alternate closings — one using a simple closing question, and another using the "assumptive" method described. During the course of the call, experienced TSRs can usually tell which approach is likely to be more successful with a particular prospect.

THE WRAP-UP

It's not a good idea to talk much past the close. Get the information you need and get off the phone as soon as you can.

The wrap-up should confirm all shipping or delivery addresses, billing information, and any relevant details of the transaction. Strive to create certainty by confirming time, date and place if an appointment is scheduled.

Many successful TSRs use an ancillary call guide that lists wrap-up statements and questions. It serves as a checklist for obtaining and recording required wrap-up data. ☎

CHAPTER VI

INBOUND CALLS

Inbound calls are your pipeline to business. No amount of planning, preparation and practice is too much to perfect the telephone techniques that will make your company really stand out in a field of mediocre performers.

INBOUND CALLS

The customer sales/service representatives (CSRs) who handle your incoming calls are the lifeblood of your business. They forge the image of your company in the eyes of customers and prospects. Training your CSRs in what to say and how to say it will reap big benefits. According to Chip Bell and Ron Zemke, authors of *Managing Knock Your Socks Off Service*, companies with high-service ratings reap these rewards:

☎ They keep their customers 50 percent or more longer than companies with poor service.

☎ They have lower sales and marketing costs.

☎ Their net profits can be 7 to 17 percent higher.

A well-prepared telephone script is an excellent way to train your new CSRs, and keep experienced reps at peak performance. CSRs who follow a script designed to *control the call* will be much more effective and more likely to achieve the established objectives.

Effective inbound call scripts begin with a well-prepared pre-scriptwriting planning sheet (see Chapter II). Whenever I am contracted to write an inbound script, I first interview the management to get a clear definition of their purpose and objectives.

Also, we discuss potential obstacles, initial offers to be made, and, of course, special promotional offers, if any. I then ask the management to tell me the benefits and special features that are available from doing business with their firm. All this comprises the research data needed to compose an effective inbound call script.

The next thing I do is call several of the contracting firm's competitors to see how they handle incoming calls. This usually proves to be a very enlightening exercise in what and what not to say, and it's easy to tell which CSRs have been well-trained on telephone techniques and are using a good script.

In the hundreds of such calls I have made, the ratio of excellent performance versus fair or poor is about one to four. For example, recently, I called five local hotels and asked: "What are your rates?" Four out of five reservationists simply quoted rates for different types of rooms and stopped, waiting for me to make the next move. Not one of the "poor four" asked: "What dates would you be staying with us?" or "How many will there be in your party?" or most important, "May I book that reservation for you today?"

As unbelievable as it seems, only one of the five reservationists assumed the role of a true customer sales representative and actually tried to make the sale. All the rest were simply courteous information givers, and provided only the information I requested. They did not control the call.

Controlling the call does not mean controlling the caller. It means taking charge by using the Statement/ Question Technique to lead the prospect to the successful accomplishment of his or her call purpose. In the hotel reservation scenario, the reservationists could have helped me immediately reserve a room in a great place at a satisfactory rate.

By merely quoting rates, and not asking for the order, I was encouraged to shop around until I reached a CSR who asked the closing question. A well-written script in the hands of trained CSRs is good insurance that your business will not be in the four-out-of-five category that lets business slip through its fingers.

The situation I have just described is often one of perception. Many people who take jobs as receptionists or reservationists do not perceive themselves as "salespeople." Inbound calls are always considered much easier than outbound calls. The unfortunate result is that many companies fail to put their best people or even well-trained people with a good script on the incoming calls. Let's look at the elements of a good inbound call script.

GREETING THE CUSTOMER

The greeting should convey professionalism, warmth and certainty so the client feels good about having called your company. This is very important because it sets the tone for all that follows.

Clear Identification

The greeting starts with a clear identification of who you are:

- ☎ Give a salutation: "Good morning," "Good afternoon" or "Good evening."

- ☎ State the name of your company: "This is ABC Van and Storage."

- ☎ Add the name of the CSR: "My name is Judy."

- ☎ Ask the prospect: "How may I help you?"

I cannot overstress the importance of enunciation. Train your CSRs not to rush through the greeting. Don't make the customer feel wrong or uncertain at the outset by making him or her ask, "What did you say is the name of your company?"

I have called companies where the phones were answered, "This is PFLARMBF." I had to say, "Excuse me, I was calling ABC Van and Storage. What number have I reached?" This is definitely not a good way to start.

CONTROL THE CALL

Notice that in the greeting, we made a statement and then asked the question: "How may I help you?" The question can lead in many directions, so the CSR must be knowledgeable and prepared. The CSR must be trained to efficiently handle requests or refer the caller to the proper person without hesitation.

When callers are seeking information, it is always beneficial for the CSR to control the conversation by using the Statement/Question Technique.

This can turn a simple inquiry into a profitable relationship that might otherwise be lost if you provide only the requested information. The objective is to get the prospect to act in some way, to come into the store, or place an order now over the phone, if appropriate.

RESPONDING TO THE REQUEST

IDENTIFY THE PROSPECT

After you have asked how you may help, the prospect will usually ask for information. For example, "I'm interested in renting some storage space. Can you tell me how much it costs?" Respond by saying, "Yes, I'll be glad to give you that information. May I have your name please?"

Identify the Prospect

It will make the conversation much more personal if you can use the prospect's name when discussing price, terms and conditions or posing qualifying questions.

Asking for the caller's name should be done in a light, non-intrusive tone that doesn't lead the prospect to feel that he or she is being committed in any way. The caller will say, "My name is Jim Smith." You have started to develop a relationship with the prospect.

Determine the Prospect's Needs

Now you can say, "Thank you, Mr. Smith. The cost of our storage space varies with the amount of space you need, and possibly with the length of time you intend to use it. Just to be sure I'm quoting a price for exactly what you need, may I ask you a few questions?"

Mr. Smith gives permission, responding, "Okay."

Now you can ask:

"What type of items will you be storing?"

"How long will you be needing the space?"

"How soon will you be needing the space?"

Providing a Sales Message and Asking a Question

Based on the answers given, make a statement that carries a sales message:

"Mr. Smith, it sounds like you may need a 10x10 unit. But since some of our units have 10-foot ceilings, you may be able to get by with less. The best thing would be for you to come down to our location so you can select the right unit for your needs. We are easy to find. We are located on XYZ Street near the outlet store. Could you come by today and take a look? We're open 'til nine."

At this point, you have established a relationship with the prospect. You have determined his particular needs. You have established yourself as a person who is capable and willing to solve problems. Most important, you have given him a logical reason to come into the store where you can actually "close" the sale.

Notice you haven't actually quoted any prices. The prospect may ask:

"How much would the 10x10 unit be?"

You can quote a price for that unit, but you must include another sales message in the form of a compelling feature or benefit available from your company. Then ask another question, such as:

"Can you come by today and see which size would best fit your needs?"

CLOSING

To most salespeople, closing means getting the prospect to agree to purchase. It can also mean obtaining an appointment to meet with the decision maker to provide consultation; to take him or her to the next step toward finally reaching the immediate or ultimate objective.

Closing is the "moment of truth" — you succeed if he or she agrees, or fail if he or she declines or decides negatively. Asking the closing question usually does not result in a yes or no, but often brings up objections or requests for more information.

This begins a cycle in the dialog between the prospect and CSR in which the CSR must maintain control. If the prospect states an objection or asks a question, the CSR must answer the objection or question, provide a sales message and then ask another question. This cycle may be repeated several times during the closing process.

Recommendations/Suggestions

Closings can often be conveniently initiated by making a recommendation or a suggestion. If you have established yourself as an expert or at least as a knowledgeable, capable person during the dialog, a recommendation or suggestion seems natural and non-intrusive. This is the essence of consultative selling. For example:

"Mr. Smith, based on what you've told me, it sounds like you need a 10x10 storage unit. May I recommend that you come down to our storage center? You can select the particular unit that will be exactly right for your needs. Could you come in today?"

In another scenario, you might say:

"Ms. Jones, based on the quantity of copies you produce every day, may I suggest our Model A copier? I'm sure it will save you many hours of costly labor. I would like to recommend that we bring one to your office for a free demonstration. We could bring it out this afternoon. Would that work for you?"

Ask for the Order

Couple your request for the order, your request for the customer to come into the store, or your request for the appointment with your recommendation as stated in the previous examples.The customer may say yes or no, but usually will either ask more questions, or state an objection. This is where a "branched" script becomes very valuable. (See Chapter VIII on Branched Scripts.)

Increasing or Upgrading the Order

In certain selling situations where you are able to actually sell or take merchandise orders by phone, exploit the opportunity to increase the value of the sale by increasing and/or upgrading the order. Once you have taken the initial order, offer the customer the benefit of any special promotions you may have or suggest "special deals" on companion products.

For instance, if a customer has called in an order for 200 reams of copier paper, ask if you may also recommend that he add a new toner cartridge that's on special this month. Or suggest that if he increases his order from 200 reams to 500 reams, he will be able to save an additional 25 percent on the entire order.

ASK FOR THE ORDER

Never recommend more than two upgrades per call because the customer will become weary of this in a short time. The CSR should be trained to detect signs of impatience or fatigue on the part of the customer and respond accordingly.

WRAP-UP

The wrap-up portion of the call cements the relationship and creates certainty for you and the caller. While the greeting is intended to create a good first impression, the wrap-up is your opportunity to leave a positive last impression.

Source the Call

The wrap-up is also an appropriate place to source the call. This means you find out where or how the prospect heard about your company. After you have successfully conducted the business at hand, you can say:

"Mr. Jones, how did you hear about us?"

These are important words because the response will be valuable information when it's time to decide how to best use your advertising dollars. It's smart business to know the origin of your business.

Summarize and Create Certainty

Summarizing the call is a good way to make certain you and the prospect have a clear understanding of what transpired and concur on any agreements that were reached. If products were ordered, restate the item or model number, quantities, price, discounts if any, terms and conditions, shipping arrangements, delivery time and any other relevant data.

If the prospect agreed to an appointment, restate the day, time and place, and what you plan to do. If you are sending out a brochure, restate the mailing address, and say you will call again after he or she has had time to review the data. Leave the prospect or customer with a clear understanding of what will happen next.

THE SIGN-OFF

Avoid ending calls with statements such as:

"Thanks for calling, if we can ever help you out, let us know."

This implies the customer is weak and may need you; but worse, it leaves the next connection up to the customer. Never put your future or power into the customer's hands. Keep the power by telling the prospect/customer what to expect: that you will be contacting him or her to provide information on special offerings and beneficial opportunities for him or her and, if appropriate, his or her business.

Finally, say:

"Goodbye and thanks for calling _____ (your company name)."

People have a tendency to remember the last thing they hear! ☎

CHAPTER VII

ALL ABOUT OBJECTIONS

Objections are reasons people give for not buying, or for not making decisions in response to your telemarketing efforts. These reasons usually stem from one or more of the following conditions:

1. **Skepticism.** At some point in the past, the prospect had a negative experience with a telemarketer, or has heard of some deficiency that may exist in the products or services about which you are calling.

2. **Priorities.** Your call may be received at a time when the prospect's attention is consumed by a more compelling purpose than conversing with you.

3. **Lack of Understanding or Knowledge.** Objections may be veiled requests for more information to justify making a decision to buy.

4. **The Need to Shop Around.** Many buyers are required to satisfy company and/or government regulations by obtaining several proposals to compare before awarding purchase orders or contracts.

Many telemarketers dread objections because they perceive them as threats to their success. The give-and-take aspect of handling objections causes the process to be viewed as a virtual minefield of uncertainty.

If the TSR lacks product knowledge or technique in handling objections, he or she will lose confidence and become intimidated by the prospect, who may know more about the subject than the TSR does. Don't despair! The remedy for fear of objections lies in good preparation and the availability of a script designed to handle objections.

Notice I used the term *handle* objections rather than *overcome* objections. I do not believe it's possible to overcome any situation where you are inviting or enticing the prospect to become associated with you. Buyers and consumers are becoming more sophisticated every day, and with very few exceptions, will not be intimidated, misled or manipulated.

Handling the objection means understanding what the prospect is saying, acknowledging his or her point of view, probing for additional information to bring the objection into mutually clear focus, and providing new data that will relieve his or her concern.

This must be done with an attitude of truly wanting to serve the prospect's need, not just hoping to make a sale. Scriptwriting for handling objections starts with the pre-scriptwriting planning sheet outlined in Chapter II.

Begin with a list of all the objections you can possibly think of that may be relevant to the call campaign. The following is a list of a few common objections; you can probably think of many more:

☎ I'm not interested,

☎ No time to talk now,

☎ I don't see salespeople, tell me over the phone,

☎ Send me some information in the mail,

☎ I already have what you're trying to sell me,

☎ You are wasting your time,

☎ I'm loyal to my present supplier,

☎ I don't need your kind of product or service,

☎ No money or no budget available,

☎ Price is too high,

☎ Are you trying to sell me something?

☎ I don't have the authority to make that decision.

Being a natural part of the sales cycle, objections fall into four basic categories, referred to in sales parlance as the four Ps. These are: Price, Product, Procrastination and Personality.

PRICE
PRODUCT
PROCRASTINATION
PERSONALITY

PRICE

The customer is not convinced the benefits of the product or service are commensurate with the price quoted. Handling this objection requires a subtle statement of features that provides deeper understanding of how the product or service can actually improve the prospect's situation in a way that justifies the cost.

For example, I recently wrote a script for a company that sells subscriptions to a weekly publication for the construction industry that lists all of the major construction products that are up for bid within a specific region of the country. It also lists the successful bidders and selected subcontractors for recently awarded contracts. This is very valuable information and well worth the asking price.

The most common objection TSRs receive when telemarketing this publication is price. The subscription costs several hundred dollars per year, which, at first, sounds outrageously expensive for a weekly publication. However, prospects are often unaware that an enormous amount of research is constantly done to provide and maintain the database.

Even more important, prospects are not aware of the true potential value of the data. Having that kind of information can vastly improve their ability to bid with knowledge and confidence on the right jobs. The investment in the publication can pay for itself many times over in the first few weeks.

The trick in good scriptwriting is to be able to anticipate the objection and provide information that is believable and understandable. It should be the scriptwriter's aim to defuse the price objection before it comes up. For the above example, I scripted the following response to the question, "How much is the weekly publication?":

"Ms. Jones, at this time we are introducing this weekly into your area at an introductory annual rate of just $450. That's less than $9 per week for all that valuable information. We can either bill you for the amount, or we can charge it to your MasterCard or VISA account. Which would you prefer?"

If the prospect objects to the price by saying "I can't afford that much," the branched script directs the TSR to this response:

"Ms. Jones, we understand how you feel. Sometimes it's hard to know how to best spend your resources. But if having the right information can improve your ability to bid with knowledge and confidence on the right jobs, then this small investment may pay for itself many times over in the first few weeks. May I place an order for you now so you can get things going right away?"

If the prospect is still objecting by saying "No, not now, maybe later," it's time to make a final closing offer with some additional incentive for the prospect to buy now. It should sound something like this:

"Ms. Jones, it would be a shame for you to miss out on all of the upcoming opportunities that will be available in the next few weeks. As I mentioned, we are offering this at a reduced annual rate of $450. In addition, if you place your order now, we will give you an extra month of service. In other words, you will receive 13 months' service for the cost of 12. Ms. Jones, may I place an order for you today?"

If you haven't convinced the prospect at this stage, you probably won't, at least not at this time. The kind and gentle way to end the call is to say:

"Ms. Jones, I'm sorry that we can't be of service to your company now. Please keep our offer in mind. I'll call again in a few weeks to see if circumstances have changed so you can take advantage of using our information to benefit your bidding process. We certainly appreciate the time and consideration you have given us. Thank you and goodbye." *Hang up after the prospect.*

The major objection to this publication is price. Its selling sequence is to place an initial qualifying call to construction firms to determine if they are really potential clients for the publication. During the initial call, if the prospect sounds interested and is qualified, an offer is made to send the prospect a sample issue for review.

A few days after sending the sample issue, a follow-up call is made to attempt to close the sale. This is when the price objection usually comes up. The prospect has seen a sample of the product, and has made some assessment of its usefulness.

The closing script must be designed to focus the prospect's attention on value, usefulness and applicability to the prospect's needs. The initially perceived high price can begin to look like a bargain when all the facts are known.

PRODUCT

Objections about the product are usually requests for more information. The prospect is not convinced your product or service is applicable to his or her needs. You have not properly qualified the prospect or you have not explained the features that will provide the benefit the prospect is seeking.

The objection gives you the opportunity to elaborate on what your product will do for the prospect. The opening sales message must not be a long pitch of every feature. It should be descriptive enough to generate the desire to know more.

If the prospect wants to know more, he or she will ask questions or make statements that will lead you to the specific area of interest that's important to him or her. It will most likely be the prospect's "hot button," and that's valuable information for you.

For example, if the prospect makes a statement like, "I hear that your machines have a lot of downtime due to mechanical failures," your focus should be on explaining that, in fact, a problem had existed, but has now been corrected and current performance is the best in the industry.

A typical response to the objection would sound like this:

> "Mr. Edwards, some of our early models were assembled with faulty vari-drive systems that did cause considerable downtime. We have retro-fitted all those early units with a new, improved system that has totally remedied that problem. Our machines now have a national service record of 84 percent utilization availability, which is the highest in the industry, and we have the statistics to prove it. Would you have a few minutes tomorrow so we could sit down and go over the data together?"

The best way to handle product objections is to determine if there is a misunderstanding or a lack of information, and then provide the right data in a convincing manner.

PROCRASTINATION

> "I want to wait a while and see what happens with the economy before I commit to any more capital expenditures."

Wow! This sounds like a good, logical reason for the prospect not to do business with you today. It's true, the economy is shaky — you personally have decided to hold off on buying that new car you need. It's really easy to accept that objection, and many salespeople do. Before you start looking for another job, let's look at what that objection really means. It could be one of several things.

1. **It might mean:** The economy is a concern and he or she wants to see how things turn out before buying any new machinery ... unless he or she can be convinced there is a good reason to buy now.

2. **It might mean:** "The kind of machines you sell are way out of my league. I couldn't afford one of those no matter what the economy does."

3. **It might mean:** "I need some time to shop around and look at competitive equipment so I'll be sure to get the best deal."

4. **It might mean:** He or she has simply gotten tired of talking with you and wants to get you off the phone as quickly as possible.

So, how can you find out what it *really* means? Sometimes, you can't. You will just have to take what you heard at face value, but surely not before you get a chance to do a little testing. Use the Statement/Question Technique. Put the prospect at ease by saying:

"Ms. Michaels, we understand your concern about the economy. We hear that comment a lot. That's why our company has decided to roll back prices on our most popular units to 1985 levels so we can maintain our work force. Many of our old customers are placing orders now for delivery next year. Wouldn't you like to take advantage of this phenomenal bargain by placing your order now?"

With this type of response, you have given Ms. Michaels some new information — a reason to place an order now to reserve an advantage. This at least keeps the dialog open and perhaps the real reason for procrastinating will come forth, or she may elect to place an order now because of the price break.

Strive to get the prospect involved. Point out that your proposal can save him or her money or improve productivity, and that it would be a shame to miss those gains by delaying a decision. It's the salesperson's job to help the decision maker make decisions by providing the necessary data and logic to do so.

PERSONALITY

The last major objection category is personality. The prospect may not like you or something you said. The prospect may have had, or heard of, a poor experience in dealing with your company or companies like yours.

This objection is difficult to detect unless the prospect is very candid. If he or she says, "We stopped buying from you because we had too many problems," this can be handled by drawing out an explanation of what happened, then offering to correct the situation and explaining how the problem has now been fixed.

If the prospect is vague or says he or she is not interested in talking with you, it's appropriate to ask if he or she has done business with your company before.

The idea is to probe and see if you can get the prospect to be candid and say what he or she is really thinking. If you can get the problem "on the table," it's possible to deal with it by making recommendations or offers to eliminate the concern.

THE OBJECTION CYCLE

The Statement/Question Technique is the key to handling objections. It provides a natural cycle of progress to lead the prospect to the closing question, i.e., asking for the order.

The first order of business in handling objections is to put prospects at ease and get them to let their guard down. This is done by acknowledging the objection or question. Use simple words or phrases, like, "yes, I understand what you're saying," or simply paraphrase what they have said. This is the "statement."

Next, ask an open-ended question that will encourage them to elaborate on their concern. This is necessary because it will help isolate the true problem. The next step in the cycle is to point out the benefits of your product or service in a way that is responsive to a prospect's objection. Finally, ask for the order.

This cycle may need to be repeated many times. Effective scripts should be written to accommodate this situation. The cycle is:

1. Listen,

2. Acknowledge,

3. State benefits (sales message),

4. Ask the closing questions.

Suppose the prospect says, "I'm happy with my present supplier." Write your script for this objection to sound something like this:

> "Ms. Jones, we understand and applaud you for being loyal to your present supplier. Many of our customers felt the same way until they heard what a broad line of machines and supplies we carry. That makes shopping easier for you because comparisons are no problem.
>
> "Just to be sure you are aware of the latest advances in the state-of-the-art in copy machines, we could have one of our representatives stop by and show you what great, new advantages are available. Would tomorrow be okay with you?"

THE OBJECTION CYCLE

At this point, you will either receive an appointment to stop by or you may get another objection, like, "You are wasting your time." Respond to this statement by saying:

> "Ms. Jones, I certainly don't want to waste *your* time, and it wouldn't be wasted if we could figure a way to decrease your copying costs and improve quality. If we could sit down together for a few minutes, it may prove to be surprisingly beneficial; and, of course, there is no obligation. When would be the most convenient time for you?"

Now comes the final objection:

"We don't have a budget for any new equipment."

A typical response would be:

"Ms. Jones, we certainly understand all about money and budget problems. Often, a business needs the added productivity and cost savings the most when the least money is available.

"We have an outstanding lease/purchase plan featuring no money down and small monthly payments that can often be made with the savings gained from using our new machine. One of our representatives could explain how it works in just a few minutes. Would you be available for an appointment tomorrow?"

These examples are actual excerpts from a copier sales appointment script. This particular script deals with 17 different objections or obstacles that can be expected when attempting to obtain an appointment for a representative to visit a prospect.

The responses are good examples of the Statement/Question Technique at work. They display acknowledgment of the objection, provide a benefit in the form of a sales message, and ask for an appointment.

The responses, although persistent, are not intimidating or pushy, and they are effective. However, no matter how good the script, or how good your presentation, don't expect to sell everyone. A good script can only increase your percentage of success. Also, remember that scripts can always be improved upon by noticing what works, and what doesn't work, and revising accordingly.

TSR OBJECTIONS

In addition to listing all of the possible objections prospects may present, consider the objections the people you hire to do your telemarketing may have. When training telemarketers, I often find they are attempting to sell a product or service they don't understand or don't believe in. Some feel the price of the product or service is too high.

Often, they are calling to present a case for something they could never afford themselves and wouldn't buy if they could. This situation gets in the way of their effectiveness. It's difficult to sell something if you don't understand it, and are not enthusiastic about it because you don't think it's worth the asking price.

I recommend that people who manage TSRs spend at least a few minutes each week with every TSR in a candid discussion about their feelings about the product or service, the pricing policy, and general comments on what type of resistance or problems they are encountering.

TSR OBJECTIONS

I was engaged as a consultant by a company that was attempting to market unscrambled movie programming to rural customers who used satellite dishes to receive their programs. This company was using a group of 12 TSRs, and their closing ratio was very low. I was hired to determine why the productivity and closing ratio was low, and make recommendations or changes as required to dramatically improve performance.

As I reviewed the situation, I found most of the TSRs to be competent and qualified for the job. The script they were using wasn't bad and should have produced moderately good results.

The product seemed to be useful, necessary and reasonably priced. But when monitoring calls made by the TSRs, their presentations lacked vitality and sincerity. They simply seemed to be saying the words on the script, but their motivation level was very low. Something was wrong.

To get to the bottom of the situation, I took the 12 TSRs into a conference room away from telephones, management and any other interruptions, and asked them to candidly tell me what problems they were experiencing.

One of the TSRs finally spoke up and said she knew there was a similar service provided by a competitor that was less costly, and when she signed up a customer, she felt like she was "ripping them off." Further discussion revealed that her company had a "package deal" that coupled movie channels with a large array of other programming.

This package, she felt, was a better value, but it was a "large-ticket" item, meaning more total dollars per month for the consumer and, therefore, a more difficult sale. After a few more minutes of conversation with the group, I determined that nearly all had the same feelings about the price and value of the product they were attempting to sell. Their mindset was getting in the way of what they were trying to accomplish. Now, at least, we had the real problem on the table.

I advised the group they had three choices they could pursue. First, if they couldn't feel good about what they were selling and the service they were performing, they could quit the job and go on to something else.

Or, second, they could adopt the attitude that price was none of their business and direct the energy they had been wasting worrying about price toward accepting the price as reasonable and getting on with the job of selling. The third alternative was to ask their management to reduce the price to a level they felt was competitive.

After some discussion, they elected to do three things. First, to track and report the prices of competitors so their supervisor could present a case to management for some adjustment in pricing.

Second, they decided for the time being, they would really try to sell at the existing prices because price was none of their business, and, best of all, they decided to concentrate on trying to sell the "package deal," even though it was a "large-ticket" item.

This change in their thinking, coupled with a few script changes, increased their results by 300 percent the following month, and not one decided to quit! In this case, the TSRs' objections were more of a negative factor than the prospects' objections.

The upshot of this example is that it pays to check the pulse of your TSRs to find out how they feel about the product, its usefulness, its acceptance, the price and so on. If the TSRs are not enthusiastic proponents of your campaign, it probably won't succeed. ☎

CHAPTER VIII

SCRIPT FORMATTING AND ORGANIZATION

The purpose of the telemarketing script is to provide TSRs and CSRs with easy-to-use documentation of what to say and how to say it from the opening of the call to the close. Depending on the call purpose, objectives and sophistication of the telemarketing operation, scripts can range from a single handwritten sheet to a multi-page, flip-chart type of document.

Some telemarketing operations may require ancillary "call guides" that display technical information, product specifications, price lists, terms and conditions or other supporting data.

If a company chooses to use a computerized contact-management database, there are software programs available that can integrate the database with on-screen telemarketing scripts and call guides.

The computerized system works in a similar manner to the manual flip-chart type of script where the TSR or CSR can deliver structured information to a prospect and, based on the prospect's response, skip to additional related information.

While the script is being executed on the computer, however, information on the prospect's responses may be saved in a notes section or placed directly into one of the user-defined fields on the prospect contact screen.

Once this data is entered, filter expressions may be used to select contacts who responded in a similar way to script questions. These computerized software programs with embcddcd scripts can save considerable time and effort for telemarketers.

Not only will they benefit from the automatic dialing feature of the program, but the task of gathering and maintaining data for performance results and preparation of management visibility reports is greatly simplified. Software is available for single-user systems or multi-station networks and is now affordably priced.

If you are just starting to use telemarketing, it is probably better to begin with a manual script and get comfortable with its use.

Once you have gotten the hang of using the script and develop expertise, it is a simple matter to convert to computer-aided calling if you choose to do so, and your telemarketing campaign warrants the cost conversion.

Whether you are just beginning and employ one TSR or have been telemarketing for years and use hundreds of networked computer stations, the important point to remember is that results are directly proportionate to the effectiveness of the script and the performance of the TSR who delivers the information.

BRANCHED SCRIPTS

A branched script is designed to obtain qualifying information, politely terminate the call if the prospect is not qualified, or proceed with the call if the prospect is qualified.

In proceeding with the call, the branched script provides a sales message, handles objections when encountered, and leads the prospect to a closing situation. With properly designed branching, the script will be responsive to any foreseen objections or obstacles, allowing the TSR or CSR to maintain control of the call.

When writing a branched script, start with the assumption that you will have to deal with a call screener. This is usually the case when calling business-to-business, but you may reach the decision maker directly. The script should deal with either case.

**BRANCHED
SCRIPTS**

The opener should sound like this:

"Good morning, this is Farnsworth Laboratories. How may I help you?"

"Good morning, my name is George Smith. I'm calling from Midway Brokers here in Phoenix. Maybe you can help me. Can you tell me the name of the person there at Farnsworth who's responsible for purchasing your laboratory supplies?"

You could receive any one of several responses. For example:

a) *Yes, that would be Mr. Hagopian.*   Go to #1

b) *This is he/she speaking.*　　　Go to #2

c) *What is this call regarding?*　　Go to #3

d) *That person is not available today.* Go to #4

Write a scripted response for statements a) through d) on a separate piece of paper and number them according to the "Go to" directive. The following are sample responses and related dialog:

1) [From opener a)] *Yes, that would be Mr. Hagopian.*

"Oh, thank you, and how is that name spelled?"

H-A-G-O-P-I-A-N (record and file spelling)

"Okay, good ... may I speak to him please?"

a) *Yes, I'll connect you.*　　　Go to #5

b) *He is not available now.*　　Go to #4

c) *What is this call regarding?* Go to #3

2) [From opener b)] *Decision maker answers the phone.*

"Oh, good! May I ask, what is your name please?"

My name is Verge Hagopian.

"Thank you, Mr. Hagopian. As I mentioned, I'm calling from Midway Brokers. We are specialists in providing chromatography accessories and associated glassware products. We're calling to introduce ourselves. Do you have a moment to talk?"

a) *Yes, okay.*   Go to #6

b) *No, not right now.*   Go to #7

c) *I'm not interested.*   Go to #8

d) *I already have a glass supplier.*   Go to #9

3) [From opener c) and 1c)] *Screener asks what is this regarding?*

"We are national distributors of name-brand laboratory supplies. We have a new, remarkably efficient marketing and distribution system that can provide substantial savings and inventory costs for your laboratory. We would like to introduce ourselves. Could you give me the name of the person responsible for purchasing laboratory supplies, and connect me with him or her, please?"

a) *Yes, I'll connect you.*   Go to #5

b) *He is out of the office now.*   Go to #4

4)   [From opener d), 1b) and 3b)] *Screener says decision maker not available.*

"Oh, all right. I'd like to call back. Can you please tell me what that person's name is? When would be the best time to reach [name]?"

Screener states time and date. Record and file. When calling back, you may reach the same call screener. It is helpful and effective if you use the person's name.

"Thank you for your help, and what is your name, please?"

Screener gives name.

"All right, Mary, I'll call back on Tuesday. Thanks again for your help. Goodbye."

Record the call and screener's name so you can use it when you call back.

5) [From 1a) and 3a)] *Screener connects you with the decision maker.*

"Good morning, Mr. Hagopian. My name is George Smith. I'm calling from Midway Brokers here in Phoenix. Our company is a national distributor of high-quality laboratory supplies. We have a unique new system of marketing and distribution that can save you money on your supplies. Do you have a moment to talk?"

a) *Yes, okay.*   Go to #6

b) *No, now is a bad time for me.*   Go to #7

c) *I'm not interested.*   Go to #8

d) *We are happy with our present supplier.* Go to #9

6) [From 2a), 5a) and 8a)] *Decision maker agrees to talk.*

"Thanks, Mr. Hagopian! As I stated, we are a laboratory supplies company and we're calling to introduce ourselves and tell you about our new marketing and distribution system. May I ask what kind of testing your company specializes in?"

Encourage prospect to talk, and tell you about his operation so you will know what type of products to offer and discuss. If you receive an objection, flip to the appropriate response.

"I see. That means you would be using items like test tubes and vials, right? How about volume? Are you running five tests per week, or more like 20 tests per week?"

Listen to response, acknowledge what you heard and proceed.

"I see, so you are doing a large/medium/small *[choose one]* volume. At Midway Brokers, we are aware of efforts by the government and industry to drive costs down and we have geared our marketing and distribution efforts to help you cut costs, but still keep profit levels up. Are you beginning to feel pressure to reduce costs at your lab?"

Encourage prospect to talk. Acknowledge comments with short comments like: I see, Yes, That's right, etc.

"Mr. Hagopian, we find that many of our clients are looking very seriously at costs — things like no longer keeping stockrooms with high inventory levels, so they need quick response on deliveries.

"Our answer to cost-cutting is to carry a huge inventory of top-quality, new, leading-edge products that we can ship to laboratories like yours within a couple of days, or overnight if necessary, to reduce your inventory. Also, since our marketing efforts are primarily by phone and catalog, we are able to provide great pricing. Could we put together an order for you today?"

a) *Yes. (Take regular phone order.)*

b) *No, send me a catalog.*   Go to #11

c) *No, I don't need anything now.*   Go to #10

d) *I'm loyal to my present supplier.*   Go to #9

7) [From 2b), 5b) and 8b)] *Decision maker has no time now.*

"Oh, okay. I'm sorry if I've caught you at a bad time. When would be a convenient time for you to talk? I can call back."

Gives date and time. Record and file.

8) [From 2c), 5c) and 9c)] *Not interested.*

"Mr. Hagopian, many of our current clients felt that way initially, but they found that after looking at our catalog and becoming acquainted with our service, we provide a better way to obtain the supplies they need.

"If you're too busy to talk now, I could call you back and explain what we can do to save you space and dollars. Which would you prefer?"

a) *Okay, I can talk now.* Go to #6

b) *Yes, call back later. I can't talk now.* Go to #7

c) *Send me a catalog.* Go to #11

d) *No, I'm not interested at all.* "Okay, thanks anyway for your time. Goodbye."

9) [From 2d), 5d) and 6d)] *Happy with present supplier.*

"Mr. Hagopian, we're happy that you are loyal to your present supplier. Many of our current customers felt the same way until they heard about our overnight delivery capability, our quality and performance guarantee and, of course, our great pricing. Just to be sure you are getting the best deal from your current supplier, why don't you consider placing a check-out order with us? Then you could make a direct comparison. Would that work for you?"

a) *Possibly. (Take regular phone order.)*

b) *I don't need anything now.* Go to #10

c) *Not interested.* Go to #8

d) *Send me a catalog.* Go to #11

10) [From 6c) and 9b)] *Doesn't need anything now.*

"Okay, Mr. Hagopian, I understand you're in good shape for supplies at present. Midway Brokers would like you to have one of our specialty items catalogs so you can see the range of products we offer. After you've received the catalog and had a chance to peruse it, we'll call you to see if we can be of service to your lab. May I have your mailing address, please?"

Record name of person, company name, company address, telephone and fax numbers.

"Okay, Mr. Hagopian. Thank you for your time. Watch for our catalog, and you will be hearing from us. Thanks and goodbye."

Hang up after the prospect.

11) [From 6b), 8c) and 9d)] *Send catalog.*

"Mr. Hagopian, we are most happy to send you a catalog and hope you will find it to be a useful tool. May I have your address, please?"

Record name of person, company name, company address, telephone and fax numbers.

"Okay, Mr. Hagopian. Watch for our catalog in the mail. You should be receiving it in about 10 days. After you have had a chance to peruse it, we'll call and see if there may be some way we can serve you. Thanks and goodbye."

Hang up after the prospect.

By now, I'm sure you're beginning to get the idea of how to write a branched script. Yes, they do take time to write, and, at first, you will probably have difficulty keeping all the numbers straight, but with some logic and perseverance, you will succeed.

A good branched script can take up to 10 hours to complete. That's considering the time it takes to list all of the objections, compose possible responses, and to type, proof, retype, test, and finally revise.

If you intend to use the script manually, place the individual sheets in a loose-leaf binder with numbered tabs that readily display the "Go to" numbers and also the content, such as, **"Recep. refers the D/M"** or **"D/M agrees to talk,"** etc.

This makes it easy for the TSR or CSR to flip to the appropriate response without hesitation. The TSR or CSR should practice using the script in mock situations for a couple of hours to gain proficiency.

If you intend to install a branched script in computer software, it's my recommendation that you write the script on paper first, and do the necessary editing before installing it in the software program.

As I have said before, scriptwriting is an iterative process. Scripts can always be improved based on experience gained through trial and error. Of course, the better the script at the start, the fewer wasted leads and the less need for revision. You will find the time spent on planning and preparation to be most beneficial. ☎

CHAPTER IX

SAMPLE SCRIPTS - OUTBOUND

DIRECT SALES - OUTBOUND

T he following script was written with the objective to sign up qualified prospects for supplemental healthcare insurance. It is presented to acquaint you with a format and style that can be adapted to almost any product or service. Notice that the script uses the Statement/Question Technique, requests permission to talk and is non-threatening and non-manipulative.

SAMPLE
SCRIPTS -
OUTBOUND

The script does display some persistence, but in a manner that cannot be construed as pushy or rude. Because it is a sample, it does not necessarily provide for all possible situations, but should provide you with a good feel for format, continuity and phrasing.

The opening is "self-qualifying" (qualified people are between ages 65 and 75). People who do not meet that criteria will usually immediately disqualify themselves. Further, this script is based on the premise that a mailer packet of information about the plans offered by the calling company has been sent to the prospect prior to the follow-up call.

OPENER

1) "Good morning. My name is Marie with Blue Medical. We are having an open-enrollment offer until June 15th for people between the ages of 65 and 75. Do you have a moment to talk?"

If more explanation is needed ...

"We have a very good opportunity for people in a certain age bracket to add valuable supplemental insurance without the usual physical examination. Do you have a moment to talk?"

a) *Yes.*   Go to #2

b) *No need, already have supplemental insurance.*   Go to #6

c) *No money available for insurance.* Go to #7

d) *No time to talk now.*   Go to #8

e) *Definitely not interested.*   Go to #9

2) [From opener a)] *Prospect agrees to talk.*

"Great! We sent out a mailer to you a short time ago about our supplemental insurance coverage. We are currently featuring an open-enrollment period. That means you won't have to take any physical examinations or put up with any of the usual hassles in obtaining excellent coverage. Have you had an opportunity to look over our mailer?"

a) *Yes.*   Go to #3

b) *No, I haven't read it.*   Go to #12

c) *I'm already covered.*   Go to #6

d) *I can't afford it.*   Go to #7

e) *I haven't received a mailer.*   Go to #11

f) *Definitely not interested.*   Go to #9

3) [From 2a)] *Prospect has read the mailer.*

"Okay, good! Do you have handy the mailer we sent you? If you do, we could go over it together. There are several plans available. Let's see if we can find the one that will work best for you. Okay?"

a) *Yes, I have the mailer packet here.*   Go to #4

b) *I don't have the packet, but tell me about it.*   Go to #4

c) *I can't afford any of these plans. No money.*   Go to #7

d) *Not interested.*   Go to #9

4) [From 3a), 10a), 12a) and 13a)] *Prospect has mailer available.*

Review each plan with the prospect and help select appropriate coverage.

[From 3b)] *If the prospect hasn't received a mailer, but wants the TSR to describe the plans, briefly outline each plan ... then ask closing question.)*

"Which one would work best for you?"

a) I like plan X.   Go to #5

b) *No, I don't want any.*   Go to #9

c) *Can't decide now.*   Go to #10

d) *Call back later.*   Go to #8

5) [From 4a)] *Prospect selects a plan.*

"Okay, that's great. Mr. Marks, you will be so glad you decided to select this great supplemental coverage. Now to get this started ..." *(give sign-up instructions).*

"Thank you so much. If I can be of any assistance to you in any way in the future, my name is Marie and I can be reached at 1-800-000-0000. Thanks again and goodbye."

After you have enrolled the prospect, it's okay to state that you are ready and willing to be of assistance and give them your number for callback.

6) [From opener b) and 2c)] *Prospect already has coverage.*

"Oh, I see, Mr. Marks. It's really good that you have supplemental insurance to cover what Medicare doesn't handle these days. What company do you have your supplemental coverage with?"

a) *States competition.*   Go to #13

b) *None of your business.*   Go to   #9

7) [From opener c), 2d) and 3c)] *No money or can't afford coverage.*

"I understand, Mr. Marks. At Blue Medical, we know how difficult these times are financially. That is why we offer the best buy in medical supplemental that's available anywhere. The cost is really very small, but the coverage can be very large when it comes time to pay those medical bills. Our basic plan is only $30 per month, but it's really valuable when you need it.

"How about if I send you a packet that fully explains the benefits and call you back in a few days after you've had a chance to study it? Would that work for you?"

a) *Okay, send the packet.*   Go to #11

b) *Not interested.*   Go to   #9

8) [From opener d), 4d), 10b) and 12b)] *No time to talk now.*

"Okay, I understand. When would be a good time to call back?"

a) *States date and time (record and file).*

"Thank you very much, Mr. Marks. You will be hearing from me on Tuesday. Just so you will remember, my name again is Marie and I'm calling from 1-800-000-0000."

b) *Don't call back. I'm not interested.*   Go to #9

9) [From opener e), 2f), 3d), 4b), 6b), 7b), 8b), 12c) and 13c)] *Prospect definitely is not interested.*

"Thank you anyway, Mr. Marks. We at Blue Medical appreciate your time. Goodbye."

Record the names of these individuals and incorporate them on your in-house do-not-call list. Further calls could be viewed as harrassing.

10) [From 4c)] *Can't decide - procrastination.*

"That's fine, Mr. Marks. We want you to feel good about your decision. But is there anything that I have failed to tell you that would help you make a decision now? Several of our other clients were unsure about making this decision at first, but after fully discussing and reviewing the benefits, they found they couldn't afford not to have good supplemental coverage. What could we do to help you decide today?"

a) *How much did you say it would cost?*   Go to #4

b) *No, I just can't do it now.*   Go to #8

c) *Send me information in the mail.*   Go to #11

11) [From 2e), 7a), and 10c)] Prospect says: *Send me a packet/I haven't received a packet.*

"All right, Mr. Marks. We will send out a packet to you today. I'll call you back in a few days so we can discuss a possible plan for you. What's the best time to call, mornings or afternoons?"

"All right, how about Monday the third, say about 3 o'clock?"

"Thank you. Let me tell you my name again. I'm Marie and I can be reached at 1-800-000-0000. I look forward to talking to you soon. Thanks again and goodbye."

12) [From 2b)] *Prospect hasn't read packet.*

"Okay, Mr. Marks. Do you still have the white packet from Blue Medical? Why don't you find it, open it up, and we'll go over it together. Would that work for you?"

a) *Yes, okay (gets packet).*   Go to #4

b) *No, I need time to look at packet.*   Go to #8

c) *No, not interested.*   Go to #9

13) [From 6a)] *Prospect has coverage from competition.*

"Well, Mr. Marks, that is a good company, too, but I believe we have a plan that offers more coverage for a smaller monthly premium. Do you have just a few minutes to compare policies?"

a) *Yes, let's compare.*   Go to #4

b) *No, I'm satisfied with what I have.* Go to #9

SAMPLE PROSPECT DEVELOPMENT SCRIPT - OUTBOUND

The purpose of this script is to enable a TSR to establish a dialog with the prospect. Through this dialog, the TSR can build name recognition, establish a relationship, gain needed intelligence, and develop qualified leads for future business opportunities.

This script is designed with an opening that is supportive and interesting to the prospects. It gives them a feeling that there is something in it for them. The sequence of the questions has been arranged to obtain the most important information first, in case the call is cut short at any time.

THINGS TO UNDERSTAND AND KNOW BEFORE YOU ATTEMPT TO USE THIS SCRIPT

1. Use the Statement/Question Technique.

☎ Listen to the prospect,

☎ Acknowledge what you heard,

☎ Make a statement regarding what you heard,

☎ Ask the next question.

2. Always use the name of the person to whom you are speaking in every sentence that has a direct question.

3. Make questions as open as possible to allow the prospect to talk.

4. Display a tone and an attitude of complete *service* to the prospect.

This script is designed to obtain the following information:

1. Is the prospect currently working with an ad agency? If so, which one?

2. What type of advertising is used — brochures, direct mail, telemarketing, trade publications, newspapers?

3. How does the prospect respond to ad/lead fulfillment?

4. How many customers does the prospect have?

5. Confirm the name of the president and other decision makers in the company.

SMITH AND JONES PROSPECT DEVELOPMENT SCRIPT

Name of Company Called: _____

Telephone Number: _____

Name of Contact: _____

1) "Good morning/afternoon, will you please connect me with your advertising or marketing department?"

a) If connected, go to #2.

b) If no one is available, go to #11.

2) [From 1a)] "Good morning/afternoon, my name is Mary Beth. I'm with Smith and Jones Marketing and Advertising. We are in the process of updating our files prior to sending out our free marketing newsletter. Do you have a moment to talk?"

a) If yes, go to #3.

b) If no, go to #9.

c) If not interested, go to #10.

3) [From 2a)] "Thank you, and what is your name, please? *(Record and file.)* We have just a few questions to ask for your input because it's our goal to produce a newsletter that will be beneficial to all of the businesses in our community. Does your company currently use an advertising agency?"

a) If yes, go to #4.

b) If no, go to #12.

4) [From 3a)] "Oh great! What agency do you use?"

Get name if possible. Then go to #5.

5) [From 4) and 12a)] "Okay. Companies like yours most likely use several types of advertising such as:

      ❑ Brochures   ❑ Telemarketing
      ❑ Direct mail pieces ❑ Trade Publications
      ❑ Newspapers   ❑ Other

"Which forms of advertising do you use?"

Record types and names of trade publications. Then go to #6.

6) [From 5] "Oh, great! You do use [product]?"

Paraphrase what the client said about the types of advertising used.

"How do you handle the response to your form of advertising?"

      ❑ Local telephone   ❑ Mail
      ❑ 800 telephone   ❑ Other

Record answer. Then go to #7.

7) [From 6)] "Okay, Ms. Green, we at Smith and Jones want to be able to address both small and large business advertising issues in our newsletter. Would you say you have a broad customer base, like several hundred, or a smaller base, like a few dozen?"

Record data. Then go to #8.

8) [From 7) and 12b)]"Thank you very much. We at Smith and Jones appreciate your time and assistance.

"Oh, and for the file, what is the name of your president? And who is the director of your marketing department or advertising department?"

Record names.

"Great! Should I send the newsletter to you or to them?"

Customer answers.

"Thanks again. Goodbye."

9) [From 2b)] *No time to talk.* "I'm sorry if I've caught you at a bad time. When would be a more convenient time for you to talk? I can call back on Friday."

Record day and time.

10) [From 2c)] *Not interested.* "I'm sorry to have troubled you. Thank you. Goodbye."

11) [From 1b)] *No one available.* "I see. Is someone from that area expected to return soon? If so, may I call back then?"

Get time and date and record for call back.

12) [From 3b)] *Not using an agency.* "I see. Is that because you have your own in-house capability?"

a) *Yes.*   Go to #5

b) *No, we don't advertise.*   Go to #8

SAMPLE INBOUND CUSTOMER SERVICE ORDER SCRIPT

The following script was prepared for a customer service presentation to receive inbound order calls from active clients. This script is an example of combining a call-in order with an offer to upgrade or expand the sale plus obtain valuable survey information for the seller's marketing organization.

INBOUND SCRIPT

Answer the phone as usual:

"Personal Resource Systems. This is Mary Beth. How may I help you?" *If customer wants to order, continue.*

"May I have your last name, please?" *If this is enough information to locate the customer, verify address, make changes if necessary. If not, get the customer's name, address and phone number.*

"When you look at your system, is it the size of a standard piece of typing paper, or is it smaller?" *This is a sure way to identify the product size being ordered.*

"What may I get for you today?"

Take the order the customer called in to give. Then ask:

"Would you like to order next year's calendar along with that?"

"Could you use a new set of tabs? They are on sale this week for $3.95."

"Would you like to try our new 'Custom Form Sample Set' that includes 1 to 3 copies of 19 of our most popular forms? It sells for $10.95."

Fill out order sheet as appropriate.

"How would you care to pay for this today?"

Pay Types:

1. Check. "I will hold on to your order until I receive your check. Please reference Order #12345." *Make a copy of the order and put in into the awaiting check file.*

2. Credit card. "May I have your credit card number, the name as it reads on the card and the expiration date?" *Note and record issuing credit-card company name.*

3. Accounts Receivable. "Will there be a purchase-order number you'd like me to reference? Is the bill sent to the same address as the shipping address?"

Check to make sure you have the customer on an accounts-receivable list and whether you require a purchase-order number, and verify where the bill should be sent, if necessary.

After taking the initial order:

"Thank you for your order, Ms.Green. At PRS, we constantly strive to improve our products and services for our clients."

1) "Do you have another moment to answer a few brief survey questions that will help us serve you better?"

a) *Yes, okay.*   Go to #3

b) *No, not right now.*   Go to #2

2) [From 1b)] *No time to talk now*:

"I understand. When would be a better time to call you back?" *Get telephone appointment.*

"Thank you, Ms. Green. I'll be in contact with you then. Goodbye!"

3) [From 1a)] *Client agrees to talk*:

"Thank you, Ms. Green. First, may I ask, what is your occupation?" *Note and record.*

"So you are a marketing manager *(repeat what the client says),* and do you use your PRS as a business tool?" *Note and record. If yes, continue with questions below. Then finally go to #4.*

"How about for your personal activities management?" *Note and record.*

"What would you like to see added to or changed with the system?" *Note and record.*

"Thank you for participating in our survey. Since you have been so kind, you are eligible for a 20 percent discount on our special custom forms, accessory pack, Beyond Time Management Tape Series, or a Time Management Binder."

"May I add one or more of those specials to your present order?"

a) *Yes, okay.*

"Which would you like?" *Add to order, then* go to #4.

b) *No, thanks.*   Go to #4

4) "Before we say goodbye, Ms. Green, since you said you use the PRS as a business tool, would your company be interested in any training programs we have, such as Beyond Time Management, for system and non-system users as well as a telemarketing training program?"

If yes, add to the order and go to #5. If no, go to #5.

5) "Thank you for your time and order. Goodbye!"

Hang up after the prospect. ☎

CHAPTER X

ASSESSING PERFORMANCE

MONITORING & COACHING

Good managers regularly monitor the performance of their telemarketers and customer service representatives. Monitoring is listening in on actual calls in progress of selected TSRs or CSRs to be certain they maintain a high level of performance. You should monitor to ensure that your reps are following the script, and that their tone, pace and energy levels are appropriate.

MONITORING & COACHING

These quality checks can be intimidating to the TSRs/CSRs unless they understand the purpose of the practice. Be sure to make all TSRs/CSRs aware that the monitoring will be occurring at random times. The TSRs/CSRs should be assured that the purpose is to maintain a high level of quality in the call process, and that they will be coached as necessary to maintain the desired level of performance. All telemarketing managers need to learn effective coaching techniques and use their coaching skills to mold mediocre performers into top-notch TSRs/CSRs.

To assure consistent and effective monitoring, managers should use a call monitoring form similar to the one shown on page 124. You will want to customize it to fit your own particular needs.

TSR/CSR MONITORING FORM

Rep Name: _____

Client Name: _____

Date: _____

1.	Introduces self and company	1	2	3	4	5
2.	Persuades call screener to connect call	1	2	3	4	5
3.	Reaches decision maker	1	2	3	4	5
4.	Uses prospect's name	1	2	3	4	5
5.	Uses Statement/Question Technique	1	2	3	4	5
6.	Listens/addresses prospect's comments	1	2	3	4	5
7.	Asks for the order	1	2	3	4	5
8.	Asks probing questions	1	2	3	4	5
9.	Discusses features/benefits	1	2	3	4	5
10.	Handles objections	1	2	3	4	5
11.	Tries to close	1	2	3	4	5
12.	Confirms order/appointment	1	2	3	4	5
13.	Reschedules call back	1	2	3	4	5
14.	Leaves message	1	2	3	4	5
15.	Says thank you	1	2	3	4	5

COMMENTS: _____

_____

_____

_____

_____

_____

COMPLETED BY: _____

CHAPTER XI

SOME FINAL ADVICE

There has never been a script written that cannot be improved. Therefore, the key to continued improvement in your telemarketing operation is to prepare the best possible script based upon the material presented in this book. Train your telemarketers to use the script. Use the script on a trial basis for several days, allowing enough time for the telemarketers to become familiar with it.

Assess the performance as described in Chapter X by monitoring and keeping score. Meet with the telemarketers and discuss what works and what doesn't work, and make changes and updates accordingly.

Manage your telemarketing program very closely, because although you may have an excellent script, the actual link to your customers or prospects is the person who does the outbound calling or receives the inbound calls.

In the Introduction of this book, I stated that there are some people who have natural telemarketing ability. These "naturals" are rare, and for the most part, you will have to take "raw materials" and mold them to your purpose.

Therefore, I suggest you screen your telemarketing candidates very finely and hire only those who you feel can succeed. If the telemarketers perform poorly, your campaign will do poorly. Owners and managers' time and effort spent on selection of proper candidates, training, monitoring and coaching will be time and effort well spent.

If you are the center of a happy, productive telemarketing operation, you are doing your part to make the business world a better place. ☎

CHAPTER XII

CODE OF ETHICS: DMA

DIRECT MARKETING ASSOCIATION GUIDELINES FOR MARKETING BY TELEPHONE

T he structured use of the telephone to purchase or sell products or services, or to obtain or give information to businesses and residences, is known as telemarketing.

Inbound telemarketing programs enable customers to call companies to place orders or receive product and service information.

Outbound telemarketing programs are those in which companies call customers, and potential customers, to inform them of offers that may be of interest and to provide service information.

For the purposes of these guidelines, all telephone calls made for marketing purposes will be referred to as contacts. Those persons who are called will be referred to as customers.

More and more businesses today are using telemarketing to meet the needs of their customers. Telemarketing is a people-oriented marketing medium that enables companies to target their products and services to customers who would be most interested in them.

The Direct Marketing Association's *Guidelines for Marketing by Telephone* are intended to provide individuals and organizations involved in direct telephone marketing with accepted principles of conduct that are consistent with the ethical guidelines recommended for other marketing media.

These specific guidelines reflect the responsibility of DMA and telephone marketers to the customer, the community and industry. Telephone marketers should also be aware of DMA's *Guidelines for Ethical Business Practice*, the more comprehensive *Guidelines* for all direct marketing. The *Guidelines* are self-regulatory in nature. Telephone marketers are urged to honor them in spirit and in letter.

These *Guidelines* are also part of DMA's general philosophy that self-regulatory measures are preferable to governmental mandates whenever possible. Self-regulatory actions are more readily adaptable to changing technologies, economic and social conditions. Further, self-regulation encourages widespread use of sound business practices.

Special recognition should be given to the Telephone Marketing Council which worked with the DMA Ethics Committees in writing and approving these *Guidelines*.

PROMPT DISCLOSURE/ IDENTITY OF SELLER   *Article 1*

When speaking with a customer, telephone marketers should promptly disclose the name of the sponsor, the name of the individual caller, and the primary purposes of the contact.

All documents relating to a telephone marketing offer and shipment should sufficiently identify the full name and street address of the seller so that the customer may contact the seller by mail or by telephone.

HONESTY   *Article 2*

All offers should be clear, honest, and complete so that the customer will know the exact nature of what is being offered and the commitment involved in the placing of an order. Before making an offer, telephone marketers should be prepared to substantiate any claims or offers made. Advertisements or specific claims which are untrue, misleading, deceptive, fraudulent, or unjustly disparaging of competitors should not be used.

No one should make offers or solicitations in the guise of research or a survey when the real intent is to sell products or services or to raise funds.

TERMS OF THE OFFER   *Article 3*

Prior to commitments by customers, telephone marketers should disclose the cost of the merchandise or service and all terms and conditions, including payment plans, refund policies, and the amount or existence of any extra charges such as shipping and handling and insurance.

REASONABLE HOURS   *Article 4*

Telephone marketers should avoid making contacts during hours which are unreasonable to the recipients of the calls.

USE OF AUTOMATIC EQUIPMENT   *Article 5*

When using automatic dialing equipment, telephone marketers should only use equipment which allows the telephone immediately to release the line when the called party disconnects.

ADRMPS (Automatic Recorded Message Players) and pre-recorded messages should be used only in accordance with tariffs, state and local laws, and these *Guidelines*. When a telephone marketer places a call to a customer for solicitation purposes, and desires to deliver a recorded message, permission should be obtained from the customer by a live *operator* before the recorded message is delivered.

TAPING OF CONVERSATIONS   *Article 6*

Taping of telephone conversations made for telephone marketing purposes should not be conducted without legal notice to or consent of all parties or the use of a beeping device.

NAME REMOVAL   *Article 7*

Telephone marketers should remove the name of any individual from their telephone lists when requested directly to do so by the customer, by use of the DMA Telephone Preference Service name removal list and, when applicable, the DMA Mail Preference Service name-removal list.

MINORS   *Article 8*

Because minors are generally less experienced in their rights as consumers, telephone marketers should be especially sensitive to the obligations and responsibilities involved when dealing with them. Offers suitable only for adults should not be made to children.

MONITORING   *Article 9*

Monitoring of telephone marketing and customer relations conversations should be conducted only after employees have been informed of the practice.

PROMPT DELIVERY   *Article 10*

Telephone marketers should abide by the FTC's Mail Order Merchandise (Thirty-Day) Rule when shipping prepaid merchandise. As a normal business procedure, telephone marketers are urged to ship all orders as soon as practical.

COOLING-OFF PERIOD   *Article 11*

Telephone marketers should honor cancellation requests that originate within three days of sales agreement.

RESTRICTED CONTACTS   *Article 12*

Telephone marketers should remove the name of any customer from their telephone lists when requested by the individual. Marketers should use the DMA Telephone Preference Service name-removal list and, when applicable, the DMA Mail Preference Service name-removal list. Names found on such suppression lists should not be rented, sold, or exchanged except for suppression purposes.

A telephone marketer should not knowingly call anyone who has an unlisted or unpublished telephone number except in instances when the number was provided by the customer to that marketer.

Random dialing techniques, whether manual or automated, in which identification of those parties to be called is left to chance should not be used in sales and marketing solicitations.

Sequential dialing techniques, whether a manual or automated process, in which selection of those parties to be called is based on the location of their telephone numbers in a sequence of telephone numbers should not be used.

TRANSFER OF DATA   Article 13

Telephone marketers who receive or collect customer data as a result of a telephone marketing contact, and who intend to rent, sell, or exchange those data for direct marketing purposes should inform the customer. Customer requests regarding restrictions on the collection, rental, sale, or exchange of data relating to them should be honored.

Names on the DMA Telephone Preference Service name-removal list should not be transferred except for suppression purposes.

LAWS, CODES, AND REGULATIONS   Article 14

Telephone marketers should operate in accordance with the laws and regulations of the United States Postal Service, the Federal Communications Commission, the Federal Trade Commission, the Federal Reserve Board and other applicable Federal, state and local laws governing advertising, marketing practices, and the transaction of business by mail, telephone, and the print and broadcast media.

DMA ETHICS AND CONSUMER AFFAIRS DEPARTMENT

In its continuing efforts to improve the practices of direct marketing and our relationship with customers, DMA sponsors several activities in its Ethics and Consumer Affairs Department. Activities are coordinated by a professional Director of Ethical Practices.

Ethical Guidelines are maintained, updated periodically, and distributed to the direct marketing industry.

A Committee on Ethical Business Practice investigates and examines mailings and offerings made throughout the direct marketing field.

An Ethics Policy Committee initiates programs and projects directed toward improved ethical awareness in the direct marketing area.

Dialogue meetings between direct marketing professionals and consumer affairs and regulatory representatives facilitate increased communication between the industry and its customers.

MOAL (Mail Order Action Line) assists consumers in resolving mail order complaints. MPS (Mail Preference Service) offers consumers assistance in decreasing the volume of advertising mail they receive. TPS (Telephone Preference Service) offers a decrease in home telephone sales calls.

Reprinted with permission of the Direct Marketing Association. For more information, contact: Ethics Department, Direct Marketing Association, Inc., 6 East 43rd Street, New York, NY 10017-4646. Tel: 212-768-7277. 1101 17th Street, NW, Washington, DC 20036-4704. Tel: 202-347-1222.

APPENDIX 1

SCRIPTWRITING FORMS

The forms in this appendix are offered as samples to help you and your organization run more efficiently and keep track of your data. These are only suggestions and you are encouraged to change them to meet your own company's needs.

1. Telemarketing Daily Phone Log

Use this form to track daily inbound customer service calls and complaints. It will track the amount of customer service calls that come in daily, as well the number of complaints.

Record the time, the caller's name and the action taken. In addition, CSRs often need to make outbound calls to resolve a problem or handle a situation. A column to register Inbound (IN) or Outbound (OUT) has been included. If an order is taken, an amount can be entered in the sixth column. Acct# and Reference# columns can be used if your company needs to track this information.

Management can use this form to analyze the volume and type of calls received, to track advertising success and to track CSR call volume. Forms like this can help you gather and organize a variety of data and information that will assist your organization in making your telemarketing efforts more productive.

2. Daily Telemarketing Call Form

This form manually tracks each telephone sales representative's performance, and gives management insight on what is and is not working in the script.

3. Call Monitoring Check List

Supervisors and managers can use this form to assess individual TSR's and CSR's performance. It should be noted, however, that call monitoring should only be done with the TSR's knowledge and permission. Used routinely, the completed form can be a valuable tool for coaching and training TSRs and CSRs.

4. Results or Reasons

This form can be used for either inside or outside sales representatives. It keeps the salesperson focused on the results he or she wishes to produce each day. The form is designed to make it easy for salespeople to track their own progress on a daily, weekly and monthly basis.

Using this form daily will produce the best results. If your sales representatives generate leads, prospects and customers, then follow up with field appointments, this form will help keep them on track.

For maximum results, write down the following:

1. Your name and the date.

2. The purpose, i.e.: To introduce my company and products to my community.

3. The intended results, i.e.: To get four appointments with qualified prospects today.

4. The time for this goal, i.e.: 3 hours.

Check your own statistics on a daily basis. Find out what works and what doesn't. For consistent improvement, fill in every day. Self-correction is the best way for self-improvement.

5. Competitive Advantage Analysis

Use this form during the scriptwriting planning phase to help you think like the customer who asks, "What's in it for me?" This form will assist in separating features from benefits, and in determining the expected or desired reaction.

For example: A reaction to a particular benefit might be to create a heightened awareness of safety or security produced by the product. Another example would be the reinforcement of the perceived price-to-value ratio of the product or service. The objective is to test the features and benefits you plan to use in a script to see if they will cause a desired or expected reaction. ☎

Telemarketing Daily Phone Log

Name _____

Date _____

Time	Acct. #	Spoke with	Action Taken	In/Out	Amt of Order	Ref. #
1.						
2.						
3.						
4.						
5.						
6.						
7.						
8.						
9.						
10.						
11.						
12.						
13.						
14.						
15.						
16.						
17.						
18.						
19.						
20.						
21.						
22.						

Total Number of Inbound Calls ____

Total Number of Outbound Calls ____

Total Number of Customer Service Satisfaction or Complaint Calls ____

Total Number of Sales Calls (Orders Taken) ____

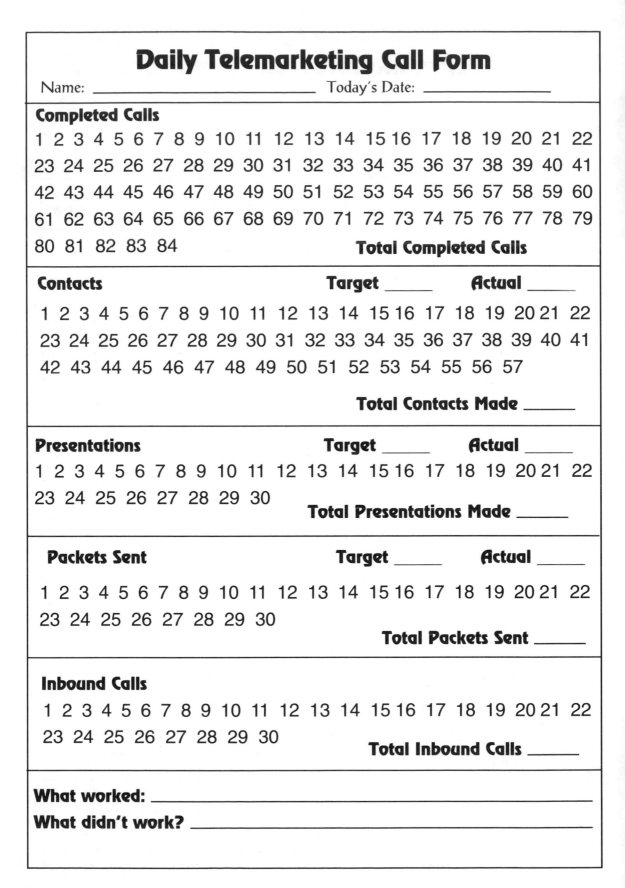

Daily Telemarketing Call Form

Name: _____ Today's Date: _____

Completed Calls

1 2 3 4 5 6 7 8 9 10 11 12 13 14 15 16 17 18 19 20 21 22
23 24 25 26 27 28 29 30 31 32 33 34 35 36 37 38 39 40 41
42 43 44 45 46 47 48 49 50 51 52 53 54 55 56 57 58 59 60
61 62 63 64 65 66 67 68 69 70 71 72 73 74 75 76 77 78 79
80 81 82 83 84   **Total Completed Calls**

Contacts   Target _____   Actual _____

1 2 3 4 5 6 7 8 9 10 11 12 13 14 15 16 17 18 19 20 21 22
23 24 25 26 27 28 29 30 31 32 33 34 35 36 37 38 39 40 41
42 43 44 45 46 47 48 49 50 51 52 53 54 55 56 57

Total Contacts Made _____

Presentations   Target _____   Actual _____

1 2 3 4 5 6 7 8 9 10 11 12 13 14 15 16 17 18 19 20 21 22
23 24 25 26 27 28 29 30   **Total Presentations Made** _____

Packets Sent   Target _____   Actual _____

1 2 3 4 5 6 7 8 9 10 11 12 13 14 15 16 17 18 19 20 21 22
23 24 25 26 27 28 29 30

Total Packets Sent _____

Inbound Calls

1 2 3 4 5 6 7 8 9 10 11 12 13 14 15 16 17 18 19 20 21 22
23 24 25 26 27 28 29 30   **Total Inbound Calls** _____

What worked: _____

What didn't work? _____

Call Monitoring Check List

TSR/CSR Name _____ **Date:** _____

Opener:	Yes	No	N/A

Opener:

1. Company and Personal Identification   ❑ ❑ ❑
   Remarks: _____
   _____

2. Clear Statement of Purpose   ❑ ❑ ❑
   Remarks: _____
   _____

3. Permission Requested   ❑ ❑ ❑
   Remarks: _____
   _____

4. Obtains Name of Decision Maker   ❑ ❑ ❑
   Remarks: _____
   _____

5. Uses Name of Prospect/Client   ❑ ❑ ❑
   Remarks: _____
   _____

Qualifying:

1. Follows Script   ❑ ❑ ❑
   Remarks: _____
   _____

2. Uses Statement/Question Technique   ❑ ❑ ❑
   Remarks: _____
   _____

3. Consultative Dialog   ❑ ❑ ❑
   Remarks: _____
   _____

Sales Message/Offers:

1. Paraphrases Needs   ❑ ❑ ❑
   Remarks: _____
   _____

		Yes	No	N/A
2.	Recommends Solutions	❏	❏	❏

Remarks: _____

_____

3. Identifies Objections ❏ ❏ ❏

Remarks: _____

_____

4. Handles Objections ❏ ❏ ❏

Remarks: _____

_____

5. Uses Trial Close Statements ❏ ❏ ❏

Remarks: _____

_____

6. Suggests Order Upgrades ❏ ❏ ❏

Remarks: _____

_____

7. Uses Fall-Back Offer ❏ ❏ ❏

Remarks: _____

_____

Closing:

1. Asks for the Order ❏ ❏ ❏

Remarks: _____

_____

2. Handles Objections ❏ ❏ ❏

Remarks: _____

_____

3. Recommends Alternate Solutions ❏ ❏ ❏

Remarks: _____

_____

4. Restates Closing Question ❏ ❏ ❏

Remarks: _____

_____

5. If Sales, Verifies All Information ❏ ❏ ❏

Remarks: _____

_____

Results or Reasons

Name _____

Date _____

Purpose _____

Intended Results _____

Time Allowed _____

Contacts Made With Decision Maker _____

Number of Appointments _____

With Whom:

Name _____ Date _____ Conf: _____

Name _____ Date _____ Conf: _____

Name _____ Date _____ Conf: _____

Name _____ Date _____ Conf: _____

What Worked: _____
_____
_____

What Didn't Work: _____
_____
_____

What I Will Improve for Next Time: _____
_____
_____

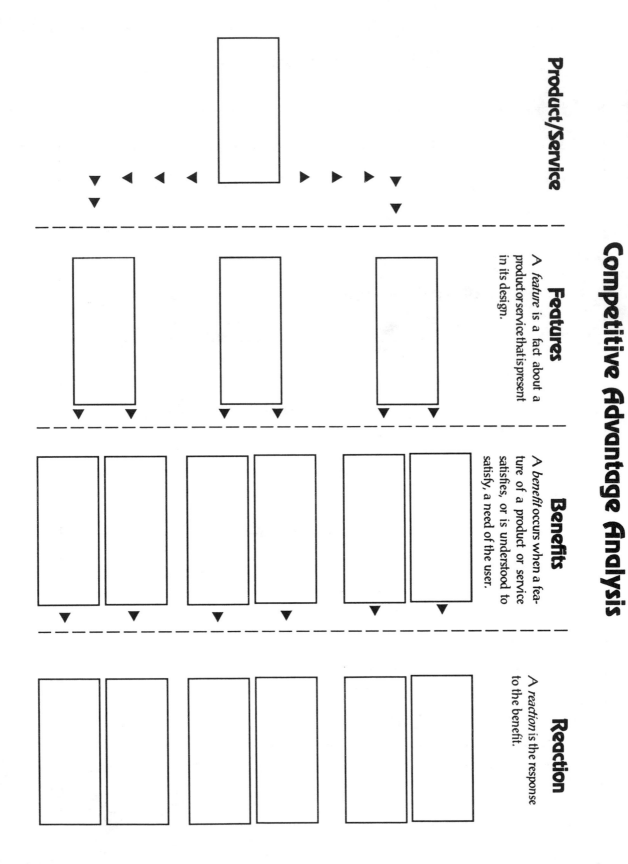

Competitive Advantage Analysis

Product/Service

Features

A *feature* is a fact about a product or service that is present in its design.

Benefits

A *benefit* occurs when a feature of a product or service satisfies, or is understood to satisfy, a need of the user.

Reaction

A *reaction* is the response to the benefit.

Telemarketing Resource Guide

**The Leading Sources
of Information on
Sales, Marketing,
Telemarketing and
Customer Service**

Telemarketing® Magazine

Telemarketing® magazine has been the voice of the industry since 1982. Alex Fraser, marketing manager of Hewlett Packard Corp., Inc. has said about **Telemarketing**® magazine, "It's the ONLY credible source of information on the industry!" **Telemarketing**® magazine is written for senior executives of every corporation. It authoritatively covers every important aspect of telemarketing, from human resource issues and service agencies through new technologies and innovative application stories. It will help its readers gain a competitive edge through greater sales, superior marketing and customer service at much lower cost. And, **Telemarketing**® magazine is the ONLY magazine of its kind worthy enough to be translated in Japanese since 1991 and soon to be published in a number of other languages for global distribution. Subscriptions: **$49** Domestic, **$69** Canada, **$85** Foreign.

Telemarketing® Magazine Buyer's Guide

Subscriptions to **Telemarketing**® magazine include the latest buyer's guide issue. This is the most comprehensive purchasing guide in the telemarketing industry. Published every December, it provides product/service listings for virtually every type of telemarketing product and service available in one convenient, easy-to-use volume. This issue includes over 700 company names, addresses, phone numbers and contact names updated annually. If purchased separately: **$20** Domestic, **$25** Canada/Foreign.

To order, call **203-852-6800** or **800-243-6002** or Fax **203-853-2845** or **203-838-4070**

TBT® — The Integrated Marketing Expo™

 **Telemarketing**® magazine is the sponsor of **TBT**®, **The Integrated Marketing Expo**™, the world's leading convention on outbound, inbound and customer service excellence. **Telemarketing**® and **TBT**® jointly train 35,000+ telemarketing executives annually.

Total Marketing™ 2000

 Given the complexity of global competition, the art, science and technology of sales, marketing and customer service has changed drastically in recent years. **Total Marketing**™ **2000** is a revolutionary new educational series designed to teach senior executives and managers in-depth knowledge of the state-of-the-art in sales, marketing and customer service, including a comprehensive review of automation technologies for the above disciplines as well as a penetrating look into industry-specific applications such as banking, financial services, insurance, publishing, computers, telecommunications and other major areas where total marketing plays a major role.

Selling Techniques™

 If you are a business executive involved in the profession or management of sales, marketing, telemarketing or customer service, then *Selling Techniques*™ is for you. Loaded with proven, practical sales techniques, *Selling Techniques*™ will show you how to turn

those difficult objections into sure-fire closes, how to find good, qualified prospects in a highly competitive marketplace, and how to sell more, every day. Published 6 times a year; Subscriptions: **$198**/year, postage paid.

Telemarketing: Setting Up for Success

This complete, comprehensive handbook for newcomers to the telemarkcting industry takes the reader from the starting point of defining telemarketing and how it can be used to a step-by-step plan on setting up a telemarketing operation, including the importance of hiring the right people, designing the right facility and finding the best lists. 172 pages with a supplier directory and a glossary of terms, hard cover, 9 1/4" x 6 1/4". **$25.50** Domestic, **$35.50** Canada/Foreign, postage paid.

Telemarketing's 100 Do's & Don'ts

This book picks up where **Telemarketing: Setting Up for Success** left off, honing the skills of the telemarketing department staff, including supervisory and management skills. It explores the question of in-house or outside agency, and how to analyze which one best fits your company's marketing strategies and goals. Emphasis is placed on scripting, sales techniques, recruiting, ethics and business-to-business techniques. 140 pages with a supplier directory, hard cover, 9 1/4" x 6 1/4". **$23.50** Domestic, **$33.50** Canada/Foreign, postage paid.

Ready, Aim, HIRE!

The most difficult part of sales and telephone sales is "hiring the right people." More money is wasted in this area than in any other part of business. *Ready, Aim, Hire!* is specifically written to help you avoid costly mistakes in hiring an effective sales staff. Twelve chapters by 12 experts will give you what you need to know to make the right hiring decisions. Edited by Miles B. Canning. 200 pages, 12 chapters, soft cover, 5½" x 8". **$19.95** Plus Shipping: $2.50 Domestic, $4.00 Canada/Foreign.

TBT & Total Marketing™ 2000 Audio Cassettes

Make your business globally competitive and recession-proof, and gain a competitive edge with fact-filled audio cassettes from **TBT®** and **Total Marketing™ 2000** educational conferences. Choose from hundreds of individual tracks and seminars on telemarketing, integrated marketing, sales and sales management, customer service, sales automation, hiring and training, scriptwriting, legislation, outbound and inbound telemarketing, and features on specific industries such as publishing, banking, credit and collections, fund raising and many, many more!

Back Issues of Telemarketing® Magazine

Back issues of **Telemarketing®** magazine are a vital resource in the day-to-day operation of your business! Consult back issues of **Telemarketing®** magazine for reference information on applications, equipment and technology, sales, customer service and automation, to name a few. Virtually every existing telemarketing center was built based on tutorial principles featured in **Telemarketing**®magazine since 1982.

Power Calling:
A Fresh Approach To Cold Calls & Prospecting

Take the fear and uncertainty out of cold calling. Learn how to find prospects, how to position your products and how to keep their attention with comfortable, quality conversation. Sample dialog in each chapter makes it easy to practice what you learn. Soft cover, 114 pages, 6" x 9". **$14.95** Plus Shipping: $2.50 Domestic, $4.00 Canada/Foreign.

Telemarketing Essentials for the Executive:
What You Need to Know Before You Start a Telemarketing Call Center

Before you even think of getting involved in telemarketing, you need to read this concise executive summary thoroughly and understand every aspect of telemarketing! By Clarence R. Smith. Foreword by Nadji Tehrani. 44 pages, soft cover, 5" x 5 1/2." **$9.95** Plus Shipping: $2.50 Domestic, $4.00 Canada/Foreign.

ORDER FORM

Please enter my order for the following:

❏ *Scriptwriting for Effective Telemarketing*
❏ *Scriptwriting ... with cassettes*
❏ *Telemarketing Essentials for the Executive*
❏ **Telemarketing**® magazine, 1 year
❏ ***Selling Techniques***™ newsletter, 1 year
❏ *Ready, Aim, HIRE!*
❏ *Telemarketing: Setting Up for Success*
❏ *Power Calling*
❏ *Telemarketing's 100 Do's and Don'ts*
❏ **Telemarketing**® Buyer's Guide
❏ Back Issue Library
❏ Audio Cassette Catalog

I would likc information on:
❏ Exhibiting at TBT®
❏ Attending TBT®
❏ Exhibiting at Total Marketing™ 2000
❏ Attending Total Marketing™ 2000

Domestic	Canada	Foreign
❏ $39.95		
❏ $49.95		
❏ $ 9.95		
❏ $49.00	❏ $69.00	❏ $85.00
❏ $198.00		
❏ $19.95		
❏ $25.50		
❏ $14.95		
❏ $23.50		
❏ $20.00	❏ $25.00	

TO ORDER:
CALL: **203-852-6800** or
800-243-6002
FAX: **203-853-2845** or
203-838-4070
MAIL: **TMC,** One Technology Plaza
Norwalk, CT 06854

Charge my: ❏ AMEX ❏ VISA ❏ MasterCard

Exp. Date: _____

Card No.: _____

Signature: _____

AMEX Billing Address: _____

_____

_____

Date: _____

❏ Bill me

NAME _____

TITLE _____

COMPANY _____

ADDRESS _____

CITY _____ STATE _____

ZIP _____ COUNTRY _____

PHONE _____

FAX _____

JUDY MCKEE

Judy McKee is a nationally known motivational speaker, seminar leader, sales trainer and author. She has trained others to successfully sell for more than 20 years.

Judy communicates a totally positive approach to selling and solving sales problems. She strongly believes that effective communication is the most important ingredient in the recipe for success for any individual. Her expertise in the art of telephone sales has put her in demand by corporations and small businesses nationwide.

Judy's goal is to make sales a more honorable, respected profession and to stamp out the telemarketing industry's poor image. Her training seminars groom professionals to be great at what they do, because she works the human side of the sales interaction equation.

Judy is the author of The Sales Survival Guide, *a handbook for daily motivation and activity planning. Also, her widely acclaimed Tele-Professional Training Seminar is now in it's first printing in module form. Judy and her husband Jim run their business, McKee Motivation, in Escondido, California.* ☎

NADJI TEHRANI

Nadji Tehrani founded Technology Marketing Corporation in 1972. The company is a trade show producer and publisher of magazines, books and newsletters that span topics from high-technology chemistry to sales, marketing and customer service with a special concentration on telemarketing. As publisher and editor-in-chief of **Telemarketing**® *magazine, Nadji is an acknowledged leader in bringing this exciting new multi-billion-dollar marketing discipline to the forefront of acceptance in America, as well as other nations around the world.*

Today, **Telemarketing**® *magazine is being translated regularly in Japanese, and plans are underway for translation in several other languages worldwide. Technology Marketing Corporation owns the registered trademark for the word "telemarketing" as used in* **Telemarketing**® *magazine.*

Nadji is the founder of TBT® *(Telemarketing and Business Telecommunications*® *), The Integrated Marketing Expo*™, *the preeminent conference and exhibition on integrated marketing. Over 35,000 top corporate executives are trained annually through* **Telemarketing**® *magazine and TBT*® *conventions.* **Telemarketing**® *and TBT*® *are regarded worldwide as the preeminent magazine and convention in the integrated marketing industry.*

Before starting his own company in 1972, Nadji held a number of important research, marketing and management positions at E.I. DuPont, Phillip Morris and Stauffer Chemical. Although Nadji is multilingual, the language he speaks most fluently is one that businesspeople all over the world understand — that of increased productivity and enhanced profits through telemarketing. ☎